Also from GHF Press

Making the Choice
When Typical School Doesn't Fit Your Atypical Child

Forging Paths
Beyond Traditional Schooling

If This is a Gift, Can I Send it Back?
Surviving in the Land of the Gifted and Twice Exceptional

Learning in the 21st Century
How to Connect, Collaborate, and Create

How to Work and Homeschool
Practical Advice, Tips, and Strategies from Parents

Coming Soon from GHF Press
www.giftedhomeschoolers.org/ghf-press/

Wes Beach
Self-Directed Learning: Documentation and Life Stories

Corin Goodwin and Mika Gustavson
Writing Your Own Script: A Parent's Role in the Gifted Child's Social Development

Pamela Price
Bullying and the Gifted

Jen Merrill of "Laughing at Chaos"
Challenges Facing Parents of Gifted and 2e Children

Educating Your Gifted Child:
How One Public School Teacher Embraced Homeschooling

By Celi Trépanier

Edited by Sarah J. Wilson

Published by GHF Press
A Division of Gifted Homeschoolers Forum
3701 Pacific Ave. SE - PMB #609
Olympia, WA 98501

ISBN-13: 978-0692374733 (GHF Press)
ISBN-10: 0692374736

Cover design by Shawn Keehne.
www.shawnkeehne.com • skeehne@mac.com

Dedication

To the families with gifted children who find themselves on an unexpectedly difficult and sometimes lonely journey to raise and educate their gifted children in a world which does not understand them, I dedicate this book to you because no child should have to suffer simply because he was born gifted.

Contents

Acknowledgments

Life can throw you for a loop, knock you down, and sometimes send you over the edge, yet you stoically muster up every drop of strength you swore was depleted from life's last heartache and trudge on until you work through the pain and get to the other side. For my family, our most painful and difficult challenges were the fruitless struggles we encountered advocating for our gifted sons at their schools. The last public school we tried to work with chose to believe our son was lazy and arrogant, refusing to understand the inherent traits and issues so common to gifted children. The effects from this experience were devastating and battling through it was the single most difficult challenge in our life. Our summoned strength and ironclad resolve were not enough this time; we needed understanding and support from others who had *been there, done that.*

With help, we pushed through to the other side of this heartbreaking journey, our hands being held by the many wonderful people of Gifted Homeschoolers Forum. The resources, support, and encouragement from GHF let my family know we were not alone on this difficult road, and we will forever be grateful. And yet, Gifted Homeschoolers Forum's support did not end there. GHF gave me the encouragement I needed to find my voice to passionately advocate for all gifted children through my blog, *Crushing Tall Poppies.*

My sincerest gratitude to GHF's Corin Goodwin and Pamela Price for their support and advice in writing this book. Your professionalism, knowledge, and encouragement are deeply appreciated. To the Gifted Homeschoolers Forum Bloggers Group, my virtual family, because of you my writing has reached a level I never imagined and you have my undying appreciation. A huge appreciative hug to all at Gifted Homeschoolers Forum.

I can't thank you enough Sarah Wilson and GHF Press for believing in me as a writer—and putting up with my tiresome amount of questions. You are extraordinary and you have my heartfelt admiration.

Much of the support and encouragement I received was from some very special friends, Liz, Susan, and Sheila. Thank you all for the long, enlightening chats about life with gifted children which played a significant role in this book. And of course to my family—where would I be without the love of my husband and three sons, my boys? Thank you for your love and support, and for always waiting until after your adventurous, daring, and dangerous feats to tell me about them!

Most important, thank you to my readers. I wrote this book with the goal of paying it forward to the many families with gifted children who find themselves having to fight to find an appropriate education for their gifted children. This book is for you and I humbly hope that it will be the hand you need to help you through the journey of educating your gifted child.

Introduction

Giftedness can be a double-edged sword that strikes at the hearts of our gifted children and their families making for an emotionally reeling and unpredictable journey. When we become weary of the ups and downs and twists and turns, especially during our gifted child's school years, we seek ways either to ease this tumultuous ride or to just pull our child off that ride altogether. But if your child is gifted, shouldn't life and school be running smoother than this?

As it turns out, giftedness—higher than average intellectual ability—seems to be a dichotomous trait beset by many contradictory forces such as perceptions versus facts, myths versus truths. Scientific facts do not always prevail over the universal myths. Intellectual advantages can crumble in the hands of those who do not understand. Innate talents may be purposely concealed to avoid the inescapable disdain of society. For an outsider who does not know giftedness, a gifted person may appear to have it made in life, yet from the inside, a gifted individual may feel as though he were cursed at birth. Good versus bad. Advantages versus disadvantages. Giftedness versus curse. All this conflict, this turmoil, has made for one emotional ride for your gifted child. Life is too short for this nonsense.

Your gifted child has suffered enough. You need to change this gut-wrenching trajectory for your child—now.

You are undoubtedly familiar with the use of a roller coaster ride as a metaphor to describe life—the ups and downs, the twists and turns, the fun and fear. Roller coasters are also a fitting metaphor to characterize the journeys we take with our gifted children, as you will see throughout this book. But, you have likely already come to realize that raising your gifted child, especially in traditional school, is not like a happy-as-we-go kiddie coaster at the county fair—it is the more like a terrifying nightmare on the Kingda Ka, the world's tallest stratacoaster with a 400-foot-drop and zero to 60 mph in two seconds.

The life of a gifted child can be quite a daunting jaunt. Much like a roller coaster can frighten more than just the faint-of-heart, so can the emotional journey of giftedness traumatize a gifted child and her family, especially during those fragile and formative years in school. Giftedness in childhood should not be so painful, but somehow traditional schools seem to take the joy out of the ride when they fail to understand and properly educate their gifted students.

The many traits, behaviors, and challenges of giftedness, at home and school, can leave your gifted child and your family breathless and fearful for what is to come next. Oftentimes, the ride can be the scariest and most unpredictable when you are struggling to make sure your gifted child receives an optimal education that meets his unique learning needs within a traditional school.

I've experienced that big, scary roller coaster ride, too, and my family is still strapped in. We've recently weathered the most harrowing part of the ride—battling with a traditional school that refused to understand and properly educate its gifted students.

I understand how you feel.

Now that the worst part of my family's roller coaster ride appears over and we are on a smoother, more predictable ride, I have learned so much in hindsight. I also have a unique panoramic perspective about this often-chaotic part of the ride. You see, I've seen this part of the ride from a few different vantage points:

- *A mom to three gifted sons*: I have first-hand experience as a frightened passenger with my own family trying to hang on for the ride.

- *A gifted advocate and educational writer*: I have interacted extensively through my writing with many others who are on this roller coaster ride and been a spectator watching other families experience their own roller coaster ride.

- *A former classroom teacher in both public and private schools*: I have also been the roller coaster engineer strapping you in your car and flipping the switch as you lurch unsuspectingly forward on your ride.

My observations, experiences, knowledge, advice, and solutions have been honed by my varied experiences as a former classroom teacher, a homeschool mom to three gifted sons, and a gifted advocate.

Are you on that emotional and chaotic part of the ride, and now you find yourself feeling as though your child's traditional school is not providing the challenging education your gifted child needs? Are you beginning to wonder if there is a better learning environment for your gifted child? Where do you go for support and advice? What are your options? Do you wish you could talk to someone who has *been there, done that?*

In this book, I offer insights, examples, support, and advice for your ride on the roller coaster, especially if you are on that terrifying ride with traditional schools. I share what characteristics, behaviors, and red flags to look for in your gifted child so that traditional school loop-de-loop doesn't blindside you, leaving you hanging upside down. I will talk about what to expect when you find yourself having to advocate for your gifted child when his traditional school is not meeting his educational needs. We will explore homeschooling and its many options and resources from my varied educational viewpoints, as well as from some experts who have *been there, done that.*

Are you ready? Good, then go grab a comfy chair, settle in and let's tackle your concerns about your gifted child's education and find ways to ensure that your gifted child will be a happy, fully-engaged learner for life. Let's make this an enjoyable roller coaster ride, instead of a terrifying one.

Chapter 1

Are You in Line for Your Own Roller Coaster Ride?

Do you remember that first moment when you were joyously watching your adorable baby and she did something so wildly precocious that you immediately began to wonder if you really just witnessed a fleeting sign that your baby could be very intelligent? You sat mesmerized, trying to replay the last few minutes in your head to determine if what your few-months-old baby had just done had indeed just happened. And your rational thought process was mingled with exhilaration, a light fog of confusion, and a bit of fear. Did you wonder how you were to label your baby's new accomplishment? Fluke? Figment of your imagination? Genius? You knew in your heart that your baby had just attained a developmental milestone way ahead of what is expected from the average baby, but you were hesitant to acknowledge, even to yourself, that maybe your child was *gifted*.

As your brilliant child grew, her precociousness continued to reveal itself, entertaining and delighting you and your family, while prompting surprised reactions from friends and strangers alike. Comments such as "She's so smart!" and "How does she know so much?" cropped up everywhere you went. By then you were convinced that, yes, your child was more advanced and much-smarter-than-average, but you were pretty sure the other children her age would eventually catch up once they were all in school, right?

When your little one's preschool years rolled around, your sassy little tike was still achieving developmental and intellectual firsts which none of your friends' children had done so soon, or so easily. What about that time you went for a playdate at the park with your then three-year-old to meet several of your mom friends with their own three-year-old kiddos? Do you remember how you cautiously, almost unconsciously, compared your child to her same-age peers? Enlightening and revealing, wasn't it? Maybe even a little frightening? Your child spoke clearly in concise, complete sentences while your friends' children spoke with unclear words in choppy one- and two-word sentences. Weren't you amazed—and just a bit thrilled—at the same time? You knew your child was ahead of other children, but you realized then and there just how much further ahead she was. And your child's off-the-charts intellectual development was not at all slowing down, while the other children were not really catching up. Was that about the time you began to wonder about giftedness and raising a highly intelligent child?

You kept your thoughts to yourself. You simply enjoyed all the entertaining and surprising mental acumen bubbling over from your child. Your now four-year old loved learning about anything and everything, devouring books on every topic imaginable. She read those books to you as much as you read to her. It was exciting and exhausting, trying to keep your child's appetite for knowledge and curiosity satiated. Your little professor—so, so smart and adorable.

And then you couldn't believe that your child was about to enter kindergarten, but you looked forward to seeing how her higher-than-average intelligence would play out for her. Those comments of amazement and sincere compliments were not as numerous as before, and although your little encyclopedia was breezing through kindergarten, the notes about behavior issues started coming home. You were a little concerned about your child's seeming inability to have one or two meaningful friendships because she seemed to play with a different friend every day. But this was her first year in public school; these were all minor issues to be expected, you reasoned to yourself. Or were they?

The next few years in public school seemed to be a slow but definite downslide from your child's years as a precocious baby, a knowledge-hungry toddler, and the highest-achieving kindergartener at her school. What was happening? Notes from her teachers, behavior issues at school, and temper tantrums at home led her to hate learning and resist going to school. What happened to the happy, exhausting child you had just a few years ago? You had to do something to turn this around. You thought it was time to carefully mention, tactfully and delicately, to your child's teacher the possibility that your daughter might be gifted. You had done some research on the topic and your little girl, now in third grade, certainly had all the characteristics. Would it seem to the teacher like you were diverting a real behavioral issue by suggesting your little girl was gifted, not just a discipline problem? Would it seem like you were bragging when you were really begging for help? Bringing up the topic of giftedness would be such a difficult conversation. You really feared being labeled as *that mom*.

Looking back, discussing the probability of your daughter being gifted began a long stretch of difficulties at school. All the conferences with educators who didn't agree with you about your child's ability, your child's falling grades and disengagement in school, the requests for you to have her evaluated for learning disabilities, and especially their refusal to even acknowledge the private evaluation by the reputable psychologist who initially, yet clearly, identified your daughter as *gifted*—you felt you were fighting a losing battle with her school. And at the same time, you dealt with the additional emotional fallout from your daughter's increasing frustrations with school and friends.

In a moment of utter exasperation, homeschooling briefly crossed your mind and you just as quickly dismissed it. "Nah, I can't homeschool," you thought to yourself. You were at a crossroads. What were you going to do now? Little did you know at the time, you were on the first loop of the big, scary roller coaster ride many families with gifted children find themselves on trying to ensure their gifted child receives the appropriately challenging education she needs and deserves within her traditional school.

Giftedness, Your Child, and Your Child's Education

Have you felt that giftedness may not have been such a wonderful gift? Has your child's giftedness ever brought you to a point of concern, unhappiness, or possibly despair? Have you struggled with your child's school to get an appropriate education for your gifted child? You may have found yourself doubting that a traditional brick-and-mortar school could provide the best education for your gifted child, so now you need to think about other educational options for your gifted child. This is often the point at which many families of gifted children find themselves reaching out for help.

You likely understand that giftedness brings many educational, emotional, and social challenges that need to be addressed, in and out of school. You also know the educational standards should be different—more challenging—for your gifted child. You begin looking into the educational options that could feasibly work for your family and your child. Private school? Homeschool? Charter school? You probably have lots of questions about giftedness, educational options, homeschooling, and possibly getting your gifted child into college at some point down the road, right? You are not alone here, not by a long shot. Many families who have a gifted child who is not thriving in a traditional school environment have all been plagued, at one time or another, with these very same questions and concerns.

We will tackle your educational concerns later on in this book, as well as offer help and solutions, but first, let's dig deeper into what giftedness is, and what impact it can have on you and your family and your gifted child's education.

Traits and Characteristics of Gifted Children

Gifted children exhibit many traits and characteristics which clearly indicate their giftedness, and they can display these traits as early as infancy.[1] As babies, gifted children often need less sleep, reach developmental milestones early, and are comparatively much more alert.

As gifted children grow, they continue to develop precociously in many areas. They may teach themselves to read two to three years before entering kindergarten. They may master skills and concepts in math much sooner than normally expected. Often, a gifted child exhibits highly-developed verbal communication skills, using complex sentences, extensive vocabulary, and well-developed ideas very early. Conversely, some gifted children don't speak at an early age, but when they do, they use fully-formed language. They are intense, extremely curious, active both mentally and physically, and often very talkative. They have a strong sense of fairness and justice, are creative problem-solvers, and can have excellent memories. Of course, not all gifted children exhibit all of these characteristics to the same degree or in the same way. Just as every child develops differently and reaches milestones at varying ages, every gifted child develops differently.

Based on the list from the National Association for Gifted Children (NAGC), a gifted child tends to: [2]

- Learn quickly and easily with little need for repetition

- Have a strong sense of fairness and need for justice

- Have a well-developed sense of humor

- Speak with an unusually large and advanced vocabulary

- Be highly creative especially at problem solving

- Prefer the company of adults or older children

- Question or challenge authority, or information given to them

- Be usually emotionally very sensitive

- Be intense

- Be perfectionistic

- Have trouble finding like-minded peers or friends

- Have an excellent memory

Parents are usually the first to recognize these traits and characteristics of giftedness in their children.[3, 4] By the time their gifted child is two years old, parents will often hear from family and friends such statements as "Wow, he is so smart" or "She is just like a walking encyclopedia." Another important point to keep in mind when reflecting on these gifted traits and characteristics and how they relate to your own child is *giftedness has a significant genetic influence*. Chances are that the parents and siblings of a gifted child are also gifted. As the saying goes, *the apple does not fall far from the tree*.

Your child may not exhibit all of these traits and you may not be ticking off every box, but certainly giftedness in children is an energizing, if somewhat exhausting, experience for the parent.

Giftedness in Your Young Child—The *More* Child

So, is your child really gifted? In her article, "How Parents Can Support Gifted Children," Dr. Linda Silverman lists early traits such as unusual alertness, recognizing caretakers (parents, older siblings) early, and needing less sleep in infancy as identifiers of giftedness. Babies can show overexcitabilities such as strong reactions to sounds, smells, or boredom. As a baby, a gifted child will likely reach developmental milestones much earlier than expected.[5] Many parents refer to their young gifted child as the *more* child—they exhibit *more* of everything, it seems.

Not all gifted individuals exhibit this *more* behavior in infancy, but many do and it can be both invigorating and wearying for the family. Almost from the moment my second and third gifted sons were born, they were much more energetic, more alert, more comical, more curious, more social, more exuberant, simply *more* than other babies. They smiled sooner, laughed sooner, and walked sooner.

The *most* child—that is what my husband and my two older sons called our third gifted son. He was the most talkative, the most energetic, the most demanding, the most active, and the most time-consuming. We admired, laughed, struggled, were amazed, cried, and were happily (and sometimes not so happily) exhausted. He cried louder, talked sooner, said more, walked sooner, ran more, read sooner. He entertained, enervated, engaged, enlightened, exasperated, and exhausted the two adults and the two nearly-adult members of his family. Sound familiar? You may just recognize your own child in this description of my *most* child. Sometimes giftedness is easier to recognize in young children when they exhibit this *most* behavior.

My *most* child is now a teen and his youthful, energetic, and curious *most* behavior is toned down, but I was delightfully reminded of how giftedness often presents itself in young children while watching a neighbor's child for the first time. We moved recently and one of my new neighbors asked if we could watch her six-year-old son for a few hours one evening. Of course we said *yes*. In one of our previous conversations, my neighbor had mentioned that her son had recently been identified through his school as being gifted and that he loved LEGO®. With that information in mind, we pulled out all of our many large buckets of LEGO to have on hand to entertain my friend's son. He arrived with his parents and almost immediately dove into the containers. Unaffected by his parents heading out the door, never mind that we were near-strangers to him, he immersed himself in the bricks. His giftedness was unmistakable—he was focused and completely engrossed for those few hours with building while asking dozens upon dozens of questions of my gifted teen using an extensive, well-above-average vocabulary that belied his young age. His creations were not of houses or cars, but of a much more sophisticated nature involving complex systems of movement and purpose. And his creations had to be exacting—he allowed no room for compromise or variance from what his imagination had envisioned. He was unmistakably a gifted child, a *more* child.

Do all gifted children have this *more* behavior? Yes and no. Their giftedness may not be as outwardly obvious as my neighbor's son. Some gifted children have been known to not exhibit recognizable gifted behaviors until their delayed development begins to concern their parents. Exceptions exist. Don't forget, Albert Einstein was claimed to have been slow to talk as a young child and did not do too well in school, either.[6]

The Earliest Indicators of Giftedness

One of the first and most characteristic signs of giftedness in young children is the early development of language skills— demonstrating very advanced verbal communication skills with an extensive, above-average vocabulary.[7] Advanced language development and use of a large, extensive vocabulary for very young children can herald the recognition of a young child's giftedness and is often a clear sign to others that your child has above-average intelligence. This was the first obvious predictor of giftedness in our youngest son. After he turned six months old, he began speaking clearly in short, complete sentences and I would feverishly update, on a daily basis, his rapidly expanding list of new vocabulary that I was trying to maintain for his baby book.

Advanced vocabulary is not the only early indicator that a baby or young child is gifted. Did your child hit developmental milestones such as turning over, crawling, or walking earlier than most? Early or highly developed mobility in infants is also an early indicator of giftedness.[8] You may also notice other early mobility firsts such as skipping or jumping rope at a very early age, something you may not immediately relate to giftedness. Having one of my sons learn to ride a two-wheeled bike at age three did not immediately appear to me to be an early indicator of giftedness. Along with advanced mobility and early, above-average verbal ability in babies and toddlers, you may soon find that your young child also has learned to read on her own.

During your gifted child's early years before he enters formal schooling, your child's giftedness may bring you more fun than fear, more delight than distress. The metaphorical roller coaster ride is more fascinating than frightening. You appreciate the positive comments on your young gifted child's verbal acuity, advanced intellectual, and mobility development, and her *moreness*.

But sometimes, along with your gifted child's exceptional abilities come negatives. Isn't that the way life is, you have to take the good with the bad? And giftedness, despite beliefs to the contrary, does have some bad. The list here can be quite long—fear of failure, envy, resentment, belief in the myths of giftedness, not fitting in, finding true intellectual peers, miseducation, learning disabilities, intense behaviors, depression, anxiety. Sadly, I could create a page filled with examples of negative issues gifted individuals face, but tackling most of these is beyond the scope of this book. I will, however, discuss some I experienced, those which surprised and confused me, and those which I have seen others struggle with, but which aren't often talked about. But for now, your ride awaits. Step in and buckle up.

And the Ride Begins

You know that feeling: after anxiously waiting in line for the roller coaster, it is finally your turn to climb into your car. Nervously, you place one shaky foot down onto the floor of the car, the car you pray will deliver you safely through to the end. Your breathing is shallow and uneven as you so very cautiously lock yourself in place, preparing yourself for what feels like the ride of your life. The roller coaster starts with a jerk, making you wonder if this might signal a mechanical defect or future catastrophic failure. At first, the cars roll oh-so-slowly along the rails, the very rails that you hope will hold out for the entirety of your ride. Once at the starting point, you sit nervously contemplating between scampering onto the nearby concrete ramp and wanting to see what this unpredictable ride has in store for you. The ride suddenly and violently jolts forward and now you are at the point of no return and your fleeting, micro-second of a chance to escape is gone. The cars rapidly reach a speed that leaves you mindless and breathless. Your body, previously flattened against the back of your seat, is now quickly thrown into violent curves on a constantly looping path. Your mind feels like it is in a vacuum, all thoughts and thinking sucked out of you by the breathless speed and aggressive movements of the coaster. You are excitedly fearful of each upcoming, unpredictable second as it races past, with no time to anticipate or plan for the next descent or curve. Suddenly, the coaster slows down, lurching your still-swiftly-moving body forward and you breathe a sigh of relief, thankful to have a single, coherent thought since the ride began. Your car melodically clanks on, over and over, on the metal rails as it struggles up the steep incline that blocks your view of your life to come, and you pray that the end of the ride is near, just at the top of the incline. You close your eyes and take a deep sigh of relief until your brain suddenly and rudely warns you that your body is mysteriously in a dangerously rapid descent. And now your ride repeats the rapid, jerking and unpredictable twists and turns from before, once again, throwing you into the inescapable dichotomy, the clashing feelings of delight and terror, of exhilaration and fear.

Do you feel that roller coaster-induced joyful distress? Life as the parent of a gifted child is not for the faint of heart. Yet, it's a ride that the top two percent of the population, the gifted, may find themselves on, with their families along for the ride. Sadly though, this roller coaster ride is often made unnecessarily traumatizing by those who do not understand giftedness, but should—the traditional school system.

Are you feeling a little jittery now that you know what kind of ride you are getting ready to hop on? Or maybe you are already buckled in and seriously considering tossing off the harness and making that mad dash up to the concrete ramp to a more predictable ride?

Chapter 2

When Traditional School Sends You Plummeting

Whew! That was some ride, huh? Thrilling, yet terrifying. Exhilarating, but daunting. Not at all the carefree, joyful merry-go-round many in society assume the families of gifted children would be riding. So why is raising a gifted child so much like a roller coaster and not a merry-go-round? What events in a gifted child's life resemble the ups, downs, and sharp turns of this metaphorical roller coaster?

The Roller Coaster Lurches Forward: Traditional School

Now, let's go back to your energetic, highly-intelligent five-year-old, the one who is about to enter kindergarten. She taught herself to read a year or so ago, and now she is doing addition and subtraction. That certainly should make kindergarten an interesting year, right? You trust that your child's teacher will immediately recognize your child's above-average intelligence and will provide your child with the above-grade-level instruction your daughter needs to keep her voracious mind sprinting as usual.

After a few weeks, the class is still working on the alphabet and letter sounds. Your child does not have any close and meaningful friendships, and she complains that many of her classmates never play fair. You reason to yourself that this is her first year in public school and these are all minor issues to be expected. Or are they?

Unfortunately, these may not be minor issues, but you are right, these issues are to be expected when you have a gifted child in a regular classroom in a traditional school setting.

By far, the single most significant issue to face gifted children today is their miseducation in traditional brick-and-mortar schools, and this causes the most terrifying twists and turns and quick vertical descents in the life of a gifted child. Traditional schooling has a way of bringing out many emotional and educational struggles for gifted school-age children. The tribulations of giftedness almost always play out in the classroom, so choosing the most appropriate educational environment for your gifted child is critical.

Searching for the Right Traditional School

The traditional brick-and-mortar school is perhaps one of the most familiar institutions throughout the industrialized world, and the vast majority of us choose to send our gifted children to a traditional school at some point. Understanding that your gifted child has unique educational, as well as social and emotional needs, which must be met in order for him to succeed in any educational setting makes choosing the right school a critical decision. No single school can meet the educational needs of every gifted child within its walls, so choosing the best school for your child is a personal undertaking, as the one-size-fits-all approach does not work for gifted students.

Once you find a school which you feel best fits your gifted child, keep in mind that its exceptional educational environment can change, and despite a traditional school being nearly-perfect, you may still experience a few unexpected twists and turns. Even that best-fit school that you have carefully chosen can change and begin to feel uncomfortable or inappropriate for your gifted child. Understandably, your child's teachers change from year to year, and a new principal can refocus the educational philosophy of the school. Be prepared to advocate for your child when needed and understand that you may need to change schools when the school no longer seems to be right for your gifted child.

Changing schools may sound like a harsh option, but it is a sad fact that I have encountered many times through my gifted advocacy and interactions with parents of gifted children: gifted children seem to switch schools several times during their elementary, middle, and high school years in pursuit of the best-fit school which will meet their unique learning needs. I am going to lend my experience here and give you some advice: when your gifted child's school no longer meets your child's needs and causes distress, and advocating for your gifted child has not made any headway in improving the situation, quickly make the decision to look for another educational option. I understand you want to give your best effort towards improving a negative situation and work with the school towards a finding solutions, but when you see that your child's school is dragging its proverbial feet or is not willing to make any accommodations for your child, acknowledge that it is time for a new learning environment. Allowing the discussions and conferences with your child's school to drag on as you continue to work towards and hope for educational improvements can keep your child in a less-than-optimal learning environment too long, which may lead to a deterioration of her love of learning and self-esteem, both which are difficult to recover. If your gut tells you that your child's school does not want to find solutions for the difficulties your gifted child is having and the changes needed in your child's education are not forthcoming, trust your instincts. I have regrettably made the mistake of not wanting to give up on a school which really had long given up on my child. I wish I would have cut the ties sooner and moved on to a better educational environment for my child.

Earning the Privilege: The Point of No Return

Yes, I have *been there, done that* when it comes to hanging on too long at a less-than-optimal school for my gifted child. We spent our youngest son's entire sixth grade year trying to have him placed in the advanced math class at his school. In hindsight, we should have cut our losses and switched schools as soon as it became apparent that neither the administration nor the math teacher were going to move on their decision to not place our gifted son in the accelerated math program.

This was a new school for our son, so we had a complete battery of intelligence, aptitude, and achievement tests completed the year before by a private psychologist who specialized in student testing, all in preparation for our son to be appropriately placed in his new school. Based on the results, the psychologist recommended our son be placed in Advanced Math in sixth grade, and I attached the testing report and math placement recommendation to his registration form. The school overlooked the testing and the psychologist's math placement recommendation, and our son was placed in the regular math class. I reasoned that though he was in regular math, it was no big deal, as long as my child was happy. But by the fourth week of school, my son realized he was the only student who knew all that was being taught and had maintained a 100% average in class. Despite speaking with my son's regular math teacher who agreed that our son would be better served in Advanced Math, the program's teacher was unwilling to place our son in her class, saying he would have too many gaps in his math skills if he skipped ahead.

For months, we talked with our son's teachers and the principal trying to get him appropriately placed. The teacher told my son that he had not yet earned the "privilege" of being in her class, adding, "I know your mom thinks you are gifted, but you will have to prove to me how smart you are." Admittedly, we were shocked by her pronouncements, but comments such as these occur much more frequently than any of us want to believe.

We pushed harder to have him placed in Advanced Math by meeting privately with the principal who surprisingly agreed with us. We conferred, talked, advocated, and jumped through hoops for months, much longer than we should have. On the last day of class, we still didn't know if our son, who maintained a 98% in his regular math class, would "earn the privilege" of being in the program. My husband

and I decided that even if at some point he were allowed in the class, he would not be provided an objective or caring learning environment. In the years since this happened, I hear from more and more parents of gifted children about how they have experienced very similar situations when dealing with teachers and traditional schools.

We did move to a new school for the next school year, but we realize now that we should have made the change sooner, even if it had meant switching schools in the middle of the school year. The toll it took on our son was not worth the effort and time spent trying to change an unchangeable situation. Yet, advocacy efforts at your child's school, when you have done your homework upfront, may affect positive changes in your gifted child's learning environment. Just go prepared.

Choosing to Advocate: Go Prepared

Switching to a new school is not always an option for every family, so advocating for your gifted child is the best method for ensuring your gifted child receives an appropriate education. When advocating for your gifted child, go prepared.

Susan Finisdore Higgins, the mother of three gifted boys, all in a traditional school system, and the head of the North Alabama Association for Gifted Children in Huntsville, Alabama, has long worked in systemic advocacy: as a lobbyist in Washington, D.C., a legislative associate for the Eastern Paralyzed Veterans Association in New York as they ensured that all public transit was accessible to persons with disabilities, and then as executive director of the Rockland Independent Living Center leading community advocacy activities as the Americans with Disabilities Act was passed. Susan has worked on over 15 federal grants and contracts to provide training, support, or programmatic innovation to persons with disabilities in school, work, and community environments. And she has advocated tirelessly for her own three gifted sons as well as for all gifted children in the state of Alabama.

From her experience in lobbying, advocating, and working to make policy changes, she has three tips to offer when advocating for your gifted child at their traditional school.

Know the players.
Do they have gifted children? Do they have experience with gifted education? What are their views on gifted education and education in general?

Know the district and state rules and regulations.
Recognize that most teachers and administrators don't know these rules and regulations.

Know where you are willing to compromise and what is non-negotiable when it comes to your gifted child's education.

What You May Experience at Parent-Teacher Conferences

A parent-teacher conference can be unnerving and emotional. Do your homework and be ready for some pushback when it comes to finding solutions to meet the needs of your gifted child. While not every school will push back or refuse to provide accommodations for your gifted child, it helps to go to the meeting prepared for compromises or unexpected and unwanted responses.

Many parents of gifted children relate similar stories of their experiences with parent-teacher conferences and their advocacy efforts at their child's traditional school. These parents went into the meetings prepared and hopeful that their advocacy efforts would influence positive changes in their children's learning environments, and came out surprised and confused by the teachers' and administrators' responses, which seemed defensive, even insulting. Again, not all traditional schools will ignore your requests or brush off your concerns for your gifted child, but many do and it helps you to know what experiences others have had so you can be fully prepared.

During my gifted advocacy, I have heard from many parents of gifted children about their experiences when trying to advocate for their children. Based on these often-occurring scenarios, I've compiled four tips for you to consider when advocating for your gifted child.

Tip 1: *"It is your child's fault. He brought all of this on himself."*

Teachers and administrators may get defensive when a parent comes in with concerns or problems which appear to suggest they are not doing their job as educators. When my husband and I went for a meeting with our gifted son's principal at his last-attended traditional school, we were concerned that nearly all of his teachers seemed to be uncaring, almost resentful, towards our son. The principal explained that she had talked to his teachers, who pointed out that our son would correct their mistakes in front of the class, embarrassing them. Teachers understandably expect students to behave in specific ways and when they don't, the student often receives the blame.

Tip 2: *"Gifted" and "bored" may evoke negative responses.*

My own experience with trying to judiciously use the word *gifted* to clarify the issues my son was having in school was met with a swift response: "Thirty percent of our student body is gifted," snapped one of my son's teachers before I could finish my sentence containing the forbidden g-word. The message was very clear: we have many gifted students and your child is no different than any of them, so giftedness is therefore not an excuse for your child's issues. Many educators believe the myth that gifted students are polite, well-behaved, and excel in school, therefore giftedness is never a reason for misbehavior, boredom, or underachievement. In the numerous comments I've received on articles, many parents have attested to the negative reactions they receive when they use the words *gifted* and *bored,* and this seems to be the rule rather than the exception in traditional schools.

Tip 3: *Request the presence of the school's gifted specialist.*

I wish I had known this beforehand. After all, the gifted specialist is the educator at any school with the most knowledge of the needs of gifted students, so her presence could be very helpful. Do not assume the gifted specialist has been consulted.

If your school does not have a gifted specialist on staff, and not all do, if you can find and afford one, you can bring your own.

Tip 4: *Use a psychologist, counselor, or professional as an advocacy ally.*

Not every parent feels knowledgeable enough to advocate for their gifted child at their school. Using a psychologist, therapist, or a trained gifted advocate or consultant to support you in your efforts to obtain the appropriate education for your child is an excellent option. During the five months my husband and I spent advocating for one of our sons at his school, we enlisted the help of a highly-recommended and well-known counselor who specialized in gifted children. She instantly knew what was going on with our son and his school and quickly determined that some of the issues at school were due to our son being a visual-spatial learner, common among gifted students. (See the *Resources Appendix* for more information on visual-spatial learners.) She also understood well the lip-service our son's school was giving us; she had seen it many times before, even with her own gifted children. Without the help of a counselor as a gifted advocate who had a personal and experiential understanding of gifted children, knew the adverse ways traditional schools deal with gifted children, and was experienced in advocating for gifted children, our son's situation at school and his emotional reactions to it all could have been so much worse. It is not always easy to find a counselor, consultant, or psychologist who truly understands the needs of gifted children and you may not find one close to you, but their care and expertise are well worth the drive and extra effort. (See *Resources Appendix* for information on gifted advocacy professionals.)

Chapter 3

Gifted Children and Traditional Schools: The Scariest Part of the Roller Coaster Explained

Giftedness in Your and Your Gifted Child's Lives

What does giftedness or being gifted mean to you? Gifted, giftedness, gifted children: what perceptions, challenges, impressions, attributes, advantages, or even emotions immediately come to mind when you see, hear, or think about giftedness? What stigmas or stereotypes come to mind? What advantages or joys do you see?

Misunderstood. That's the first word that comes to mind for me. Giftedness is so misunderstood in our world today. My personal journey with my own gifted children has been full of painful and confusing misunderstandings causing huge disconnects in my children's education resulting in their miseducation. Making the ride unnecessarily rough are the attitudes, reactions, and actions of those who do not understand giftedness. Depending on where you are on your roller coaster ride with your gifted child and how thrilling or terrifying it has been, your ideas and thoughts about giftedness will likely reflect your own personal experiences with giftedness—the good and the bad, the twists and the turns.

Giftedness in a Traditional Brick-and-Mortar School

Whatever your thoughts and feelings are about giftedness, if your child is in a traditional brick-and-mortar school, you may be dealing with, possibly not too successfully, the views of your child's teachers, the administration, even your state about giftedness and gifted education.

What is your child's school's attitude towards gifted learners? Does the school have a gifted students program? If your child is receiving her education in the regular classroom, what accommodations are being made to accelerate your child, differentiate her education, or allow her to grade skip? Do the school educators understand the many aspects of gifted children? Do they *get gifted?* The answer is important because if your child's school does not understand, really understand, all the educational, social, and emotional needs of your gifted child, as well as the traits and characteristics of gifted children, your roller coaster ride can quickly become painfully turbulent. The understanding of and attitude towards gifted learners by your child's school has the unparalleled ability to make your roller coaster ride smooth and exciting, or terrifying and painful. Knowing how your child's school feels about and deals with gifted learners is crucial.

I'm sure you are well aware of the fallacious stereotype of a gifted student to which many people cling—that of the smart, school-is-a-breeze, high-achieving, well-behaved and popular student. If we were to ask most anyone in society who has not had experience with or real knowledge of gifted children to describe a gifted student, they would most likely answer with adjectives like smart, well-behaved, successful, and high-achieving. If we were to complain to these same people that our child was bored in school, we would likely be met with responses such as, "It will be more challenging for him later, just you wait" or "Why not just let her have an easy year in school this year?"

If we asked those same people how they felt about funding and support for special, public school programming for gifted students, most likely their opinions would derive from their beliefs of the fallacious stereotype and myths which directly contribute to the dismal state—both educationally and emotionally—our gifted children find themselves in today. Too many in society believe that the stereotypical enthusiastic, motivated, high-achieving student breezing his way through school on his way to a wonderful college scholarship does not need extra educational programming, funding, or support. The deeply-held belief in these erroneous myths and stereotypes, and the adherence to the inaccurate beliefs of the traits and needs of gifted learners, hinder or totally obstruct our gifted children from being able to reach their full potential in brick-and-mortar schools.

The Myths and Misunderstandings of Giftedness

Misunderstanding is the element about giftedness which seems to have the most impact on our gifted children. Persistent misunderstandings of what exactly giftedness is and how it presents perpetuate themselves despite the research data and professional studies which patently prove them wrong. My personal favorite myth, or should I say un-favorite, is: *All gifted children are smart, high achievers, and need no extra help at school. They can fend for themselves.*

Why would anyone believe that any student should be left to fend for herself? As an educator, I believe that all children need to learn and progress at their own pace in school whether that be slower, faster, deeper, or differentiated based on their learning style and ability level. Is it ever ethically or morally right to neglect the education of any student population in school? Or to ignore a child's educational needs just because you think they can teach themselves all they need to learn without support or services? How is this a sound educational philosophy?

Some other prolific myths:[1]

1. Gifted kids are all high achievers and maintain good grades.

2. Gifted kids all come from upper- and upper-middle class families.

3. Gifted kids are not born that way; they have been hot-housed by pushy parents (the "nature versus nurture" debate).

4. *All* children are gifted.

5. Gifted learners do fine in the regular classroom.

6. Honors and AP courses are gifted programming.

7. Gifted programs are elitist, a reward for those who already have the advantage of being smarter.

These myths and misunderstandings have proven to be tragic for the education of our gifted children in traditional schools. Too many of those who hold the educational purse strings unfortunately also believe in these myths, or use them to defend their choice to underfund or un-fund gifted programs in our public schools. "Funding is critical and sorely lacking for gifted education, but funding by itself is not enough without an understanding of gifted kids and their educational needs. Our legislators and state and federal governments can't appropriately decide how that funding should be spent without understanding the problem and of course, the misperceptions and myths surrounding gifted education frequently get in the way of understanding the nature of this particular problem," explains Melissa Bilash, the founder of Advocacy and Consulting for Education in Wayne, Pennsylvania, which offers advocacy services to assist parents and caregivers in securing a setting where their student can thrive, be happy, and become an integral participant in the classroom. She is also the founder of The Grayson School, a non-profit, independent private school for gifted students outside of Philadelphia, Pennsylvania. Melissa is one of only 100 people in the United States to have successfully completed the nationally recognized and intense training program, Special Education Advocates Training (SEAT), which is the only federal training program that exists to date.

Along with the lack of funding, federal education programs such as No Child Left Behind and Race to the Top have worked together to be the educational scourge that have kept our gifted children from reaching their full potential in school. In the last ten to fifteen years, we have seen a steady decline in the quality and quantity of gifted programs in our schools. This has led to some serious and unfortunate trends among our gifted learners like underachievement, depression, and dropping out of school. In ever-increasing numbers, our gifted learners have been leaving traditional schools in search of a better educational fit in which they can survive and thrive. Charter schools, magnet programs, and private schools have sometimes been able to provide a better and more appropriate education for some underserved gifted learners who left the regular classroom. When these educational alternatives are not financially feasible or a good fit educationally for gifted learners, homeschooling has proven to be an excellent educational option.

Where the Traditional Classroom Fails Our Gifted Learners

Gifted children are a unique student population whose learning needs require comprehensive and differentiated educational instruction compared to more typical students and same-age peers. The traditional American school system, for the most part, has failed to meet the specific learning needs of our gifted learners since we won the space race in the 1960s through a national concerted effort to nurture high-achievers in math and science.[2] Since then, our educational system has subsequently provided a less-than-optimal education for our gifted children.

In recent history, federal educational initiatives have not adequately provided for a comprehensive gifted education for our gifted learners. In fact, some federal initiatives have caused a drastic decline in funding and focus for gifted programs by diverting the emphasis in education to one that has all children meeting minimum proficiency standards that may or may not be appropriate or realistic for all students. Parents of gifted learners have had to advocate at schools, fight school systems, and lobby legislators just to try to develop an awareness of the kinds of educational services their children need. All of that takes time—sometimes years—to get the education their children require to fulfill their potential. As a result, many parents of gifted children are forced to seek alternatives for the education of their gifted children such as private schools, online programs, and homeschooling. This lack of federal and state support for gifted education can be blamed, in large part, to the influence of the widespread and much-believed myths and misunderstandings surrounding giftedness and gifted learners in school.

Myth: *All gifted children are smart and don't need any extra help; they can fend for themselves.*

Of the many gifted myths, this one seems to have a stranglehold on our government's and school systems' rationale to not provide the specialized education our gifted children require to progress educationally and reach their potential. Too many people who control the educational budgets in America feel that any type of gifted education is a luxury, not a necessity. And many school systems provide just lip service to parents of gifted students and the public in regard to their efforts towards helping gifted learners reach their potential. But universally, most school systems fail to provide what gifted students need to learn and succeed in school. In the same vein, if this myth is true, then do we rightfully assume that gifted children can reach their academic and lifelong potential without an appropriate or challenging education?

Myth: *All gifted children are high achievers; they make good grades and excel in school.*

What about the predominant myth that all gifted children excel in school? For twice-exceptional (2e) gifted children, those who are both gifted and have a learning difference, this one can be the most injurious when their learning differences mask their giftedness. Schools focus on remediating gifted 2e children's learning weaknesses, then leaving them unchallenged in areas where they can excel. The concerning prevalence of educational underachievement by gifted students, the common incidence of depression among the gifted, and the surprisingly high dropout rates among gifted students should demonstrate that this is truly a myth and one that should not influence any educational decisions regarding gifted students. Yet, it has done just that with significantly negative results, as statistics have shown.

> *While the nation's lowest-achieving youngsters made rapid gains from 2000 to 2007, the performance of top students was languid. Children at the tenth percentile of achievement (the bottom 10 percent of students) have shown solid progress in fourth-grade reading and math and eighth-grade math since 2000, but those at the 90th percentile (the top 10 percent) have made minimal gains.[3]*

If one believes these myths to be true and that comprehensive gifted education in our public schools is not necessary to properly educate our gifted children, then how do we explain these recent educational data on gifted learners showing the opposite of the assumed educational progress gifted learners should be exhibiting?

Fact: *Gifted Students Have a Higher Dropout Rate*

Professional research studies and educational statistics in the last two to three decades all paint a bleak picture of the educational gains made by gifted students. Statistically, gifted students drop out of school at the same rate or higher than non-gifted students, and "researchers estimate that between 18 percent and 25 percent of gifted students drop out of school."[4] According to James Zabloski's study, *Gifted Dropouts: A Phenomenological Study* (April 2010), despite factors such as cultural background and socioeconomic status, the gifted dropouts in this study reported, across the board, that boredom in school, desire for a challenging curriculum, and a desire for new information were all factors in their decision to drop out.[5]

Fact: *A Disproportionate Percentage of the Prison Population is Gifted*

Additional grim educational statistics reveal the failure of our school systems to meet the needs of our gifted students, resulting in dire consequences, especially among minorities and children from the lower socioeconomic strata. In her book, *Gifted Grown Ups: The Mixed*

Blessings of Extraordinary Potential, Marylou Kelly Streznewski states that gifted people may make up as much as 20 percent of the prison population.[6] Taking into consideration that approximately two percent of the general population is gifted, this data shows that gifted individuals represent a much higher percentage in our prison population. Along with the proportionally higher gifted population in prison, consider this appalling educational phenomena called the *school to prison pipeline*: Activists trying to address this educational issue have said the cause is inadequacies in our educational system, whereby children in school, as early as preschool, are being pushed into prison by the school system's failure to identify and address the educational, emotional, and social needs of these children.[7] How many of the disproportionately large number of incarcerated gifted individuals were part of the *school to prison pipeline* because they were also gifted students who were never identified or their learning needs as a gifted student were never met?[8]

The traditional school system has failed too many of our gifted students resulting in disastrous outcomes for our gifted children, but those sobering realities are not only educational, they are emotional and social as well—all equally devastating for them and for society. Yes, gifted students do suffer educationally, socially, and emotionally from being miseducated and neglected in our schools.

Fact: *Lack of Gifted Education Leads to Social and Emotional Issues*

Without comprehensive gifted programs in traditional schools, gifted children often struggle to find like-minded peers, and then find themselves outliers in the regular classroom which can easily set them up as victims of bullying. It is believed that giftedness and its inherent traits naturally put gifted students at a higher risk for being bullied in school according to Sandra G. Boodman's article, "Gifted and Tormented."[9] Ms. Boodman cited several studies and experts supporting the link between being the victim of chronic bullying in school and violent behavior. Also, being the victim of chronic bullying can and does lead to most teenage suicides. Comprehensive and challenging gifted programs in our schools where gifted students can safely learn and socialize among like-minded peers could very likely prevent our gifted children from the tragedies of dropping out of school, violent behavior, and suicide.

Clearly, without the critically-needed comprehensive gifted programs in traditional schools, gifted students, in record numbers, are struggling to thrive in regular classrooms ill-equipped to meet their unique educational, social, and emotional needs. This miseducation of our gifted children has proven to lead to sobering and disastrous consequences which adversely affect our gifted children as well as all of society. Myths abound about gifted students, and when traditional schools fail our high-achievers, we all lose. (See *Resources Appendix* for more information on gifted underachievement.)

Homeschooling: An Excellent Education Option for Gifted Learners

For decades, our gifted children have suffered from educational, social, and emotional neglect in our traditional school system. They have received a much-less-than-adequate education which has been proven to lead to significant and tragic resultant situations. The loss of the immense potential this high-ability student population can bring to the betterment of our world hurts us all, as would the needless loss of any human's potential. But the loss of their own self-concept and their shattered self-esteem are the most devastating losses a gifted child can suffer, caused from the widespread educational negligence seen throughout our school systems today.

Although gifted advocacy, on local, national, and worldwide levels, has seen positive and promising results, in many ways, it has been too little, too late for far too many gifted children. Giving up on traditional schools' commitment and ability to properly educate the gifted, gifted students and their families have turned to homeschooling in ever-increasing numbers. Homeschooling has seen a dramatic increase in the number of students choosing this educational alternative.[10] Although not a large amount of research or statistical data on gifted homeschoolers as a student population exists, significant anecdotal evidence supports the belief that gifted learners are possibly the largest student population recently turning to homeschooling in order to meet their unique learning needs, and homeschooling has proven to be an excellent educational choice for our gifted children.[11] Statistics have proven that homeschooled children are outperforming traditional school children on standardized achievement tests, and colleges and universities are increasingly actively recruiting homeschooled students.[12]

With the exceptional track record homeschooling has justifiably earned, are you ready to consider homeschooling for your gifted child? Not yet sure?

In the next chapter I will discuss the critical role of the teacher in your gifted child's life. Teachers don't always recognize or understand the traits or behaviors of gifted children, nor do they often know how to meet the emotional, social, and educational needs of a gifted student. As a former classroom teacher, I admit I was once one of those teachers who didn't *get gifted.*

Chapter 4

Teachers and Giftedness: We Don't Always *Get It*

Oh, the gifted traits I never knew, the giftedness I overlooked, and the gifted students I didn't see. Yes, as a new teacher, I was unfortunately part of the large population of teachers who were offered appallingly little information in teacher training programs about giftedness in children. Only now, after being on my own eye-opening roller coaster ride with my own gifted sons, do I think about the students I might have overlooked because I was simply taught to recognize the high-achieving students as those who might be gifted.

Taller or Shorter

I just may have missed Lawrence. As a new teacher, I was observed by my principal several times during my first year of teaching. During one such observation, I was teaching the kindergarten math skill of taller or shorter. It was readily mastered by kindergarteners, which is exactly why I chose to teach it during the scheduled observation by my principal. As the lesson proceeded, every student easily grasped the concept and produced the exact outcome I was expecting—except Lawrence. Lawrence was an energetic and inquisitive child who either nailed a concept or skill with flying colors, or failed miserably. With the concept of taller or shorter, it was the latter. While my principal sat typing away on her laptop filling in the blanks of my evaluation, I tried to help Lawrence grasp taller or shorter by using objects he was familiar with including getting him to think about his mother who was a tall woman. In a last, desperate attempt, I had Lawrence stand side-by-side with me while I pretended to be his mother. I put my arm around Lawrence and asked him who was taller—me, as his stand-in mother, or himself. Lawrence looked up at me with an exasperated, almost angry expression and said loudly and firmly, "My mom is not taller and she is not shorter, she is just FAT!"

Many gifted children, especially those with strong visual-spatial strengths, often grasp the bigger idea while skipping over the easiest, most simple details or skills. Had Lawrence already moved on, ahead of me and the rest of the class? Had he already mastered the simple concept of taller or shorter and was moving on to bigger and more complex ideas and concepts? Was he exasperated with me for repeatedly asking him to produce a simple, exact answer he already knew when he really just wanted to know more about the tallest object in the world or the shortest human to have ever lived, or more advanced concepts such as deeper or shallower? As a teacher, all I needed was that exact answer to tick off that box and when he didn't deliver, he failed and I failed. Looking back, Lawrence really didn't fail, but perhaps I did. As a teacher, I may have failed to recognize that he was gifted, that he wasn't behind in school, he was actually ahead.

Why Teachers Don't *Get Gifted*

Through my involvement with advocating for gifted children, I've had many conversations with parents of gifted kids, and in nearly every conversation, I hear the same catchphrase used over and over by parents when talking about their child's experience with their regular classroom teacher. The phrase? *They just don't get gifted!*

As mentioned before, gifted students have become the victims of the myths, misunderstandings, and stereotypes surrounding giftedness. All of these fallacies proliferate when teachers are not given accurate information about giftedness and are not properly trained to meeting the unique learning needs of gifted students. This lack of accurate information and training inhibits recognition and identification of gifted students in school. When teachers believe these myths about gifted students, many gifted students who do not fit the stereotype of the successful, A+ student, get overlooked, go unidentified, and are subsequently miseducated. For the teacher in the classroom, tight educational budgets, focus on every student meeting basic, grade-level proficiency standards, and demands and expectations surrounding standardized testing all take priority over making efforts to differentiate the curriculum to meet the academic level of a gifted student in a teacher's classroom. Of course, this is not true for all teachers, but it is true for the many teachers who are overwhelmed with other educational demands on their time in the classroom, and those who assume that gifted students are all excellent students who are just fine being undereducated in the classroom.

Susan Bacon is a former classroom teacher with many years of experience teaching gifted and regular education students in elementary through high school in the public school systems of Missouri, Iowa, and Alabama. She is now the director of The Franklin School, an educational center "offering classes, consulting, a library, transcripts, field trips, and activities for homeschoolers." Ms. Bacon founded The Franklin School fifteen years ago while homeschooling her own two children through high school. Ms. Bacon has this to say about the education of gifted students in traditional schools:

> *In the classroom, when I taught in public school, I continuously watched as gifted children waited for others to finish or grasp a concept, reading books silently at their desk while waiting for others to finish an assignment, drawing pictures or doodles on small pieces of paper to entertain themselves while waiting for others to pay attention, or becoming a discipline problem because of boredom. If they become a discipline problem, you not only have a bunch of wasted hours that could have been constructive educational time, but you begin to have some self-esteem problems. I think a gifted child getting in trouble all the time begins to focus more on that, [rather] than the fact that they have much to offer intellectually speaking.*

Dr. Gail Post, a psychologist who works with and advocates for gifted children, gives four reasons why many teachers do not get gifted and gifted children are "so frequently overlooked, undereducated, and unstimulated": competing demands; inadequate training; low priority; and attitudes, stereotypes, and resentment.[1]

Parents, teachers, and educational and mental health professionals who do get gifted know and understand that our gifted children are creative thinkers and complex learners, that they are intense and passionate, have a strong sense of fairness and morality, are very sensitive emotionally, and have unique educational needs which must be met in order to be successful in the classroom. But when the adults who are in charge of your child's education don't *get gifted*, the subsequent damaging effects on a gifted child from miseducation can be long-lasting and even permanent.

As Melissa Bilash, the founder of both Advocacy & Consulting for Education and The Grayson School puts so clearly:

> *Yes, gifted education needs money; but we also need people to "get" it: teachers, guidance counselors, principals, superintendents, state legislators, and yes, parents—of gifted and typical kids! We need a change in our societal understanding of what "gifted" means, which does require a lot of uncomfortable conversations, where as advocates and parents, we have to speak up about where we see misconceptions in play.*

I Didn't *Get It.* I Didn't *Get Gifted.*

Being an educator was an absolutely perfect fit for me. Every aspect thrilled me—my love for children, the ability to be creative, and most important, the opportunity to make a real difference in the life of a child. I was so proud and excited to be a part of this fellowship of educators, of academia. I felt like I had just won the career lottery.

Given the passion and enthusiasm I had for educating children, I was soon tagged as an exceptional teacher which led to added, high-profile responsibilities such as being given students no other teacher could reach and becoming a mentor teacher, all within my first three years. But guess what? Despite my expertise and excellent reputation, I still didn't understand what I should have understood about gifted children like Lawrence.

During the course of a teacher's career, many different types of learners come through those classroom doors. Unconsciously, we teachers may mentally categorize our students into groups based solely by their classroom performance. Those students who catch on easily and quickly to the skills and concepts being taught are the bright and conscientious students. Those students who are slower to master new skills and concepts just need more help and to work harder. Seems as though those are good, logical conclusions, but as parents of gifted children we know gifted children do not always fit into those quintessential student profiles and categories.

During my early years as a teacher, if I had been asked to identify the gifted students in my classroom, I would have quickly listed all of the children who consistently mastered concepts easily and learned new skills quickly. During my teacher education, I spent one hour of one class period learning about gifted learners and the traits to look for in the classroom. Only the stereotypical traits—masters skills quickly, often asks questions, enthusiastic learner, and finishes work early—were presented and discussed. At that time, my mind quickly formed the vision of a young gifted child sitting at his classroom desk, sitting up straight, hands folded on top of his desk, astutely paying attention to every word the teacher uttered, and repeatedly shooting his hand up in the air to answer every question the teacher asked. I was never told that the student sitting in my classroom who spends the day looking out the window or creatively doodling in her workbook could be a gifted student. I was never trained to recognize that the student who failed to turn in homework, left classwork incomplete, and forgot schoolwork deadlines could be a gifted learner. And the student who, despite all of my attempts at remediation, still had failing grades—I would probably have never considered him as being gifted. Even as a highly respected mentor teacher, I did not understand all that I should have about giftedness. I just didn't *get it*.

If your gifted child is sitting in a regular classroom for the majority of his instructional time, does his regular teacher understand your child's needs as a gifted learner? Your child may have the teacher every parent requests because she is just that good, but if she doesn't understand the truths and facts about gifted children, your child may not be receiving an appropriately challenging education.

Recognizing and Identifying Gifted Students

As we've seen, teachers can often overlook the gifted child when other demands take priority, but how does this classroom situation affect the recognition and identification of gifted students? Most often, gifted students go unrecognized and unidentified when teachers are inadequately trained to recognize, understand, and teach gifted learners. Not surprisingly, many teachers, as well as counselors and principals, are looking for that student who fits the largely fictitious stereotype of the high-achieving student as a potentially gifted learner.

Learning differences and other issues such as ADD, ADHD, dyslexia, visual-spatial abilities, underachievement, perfectionism, and autism/Asperger's syndrome often coexist with giftedness, acting to mask giftedness and confound identification. When a child is gifted and also has a coexisting learning difference, he is said to be twice-exceptional or 2e. Teachers who lack accurate information about gifted learners may fail to understand that a gifted student can be both gifted and learning disabled or gifted and underachieving. As these traits and learning differences are not readily associated with giftedness, and many of them hinder the expected high-achieving performance of a gifted student, educators fail to recognize a student as being potentially gifted, so those students remain unidentified and miseducated.

Two of my sons' giftedness was veiled by their visual-spatial thinking which directly conflicted with traditional school's timeworn educational methods, though gifted identification for them would have been a welcomed revelation in their early education. Most assuredly, many of our questions and concerns about their education would have been answered.

Unrecognized Genius—Still Not Fitting the Stereotype

The majority of gifted children do not fit the stereotype of a gifted student breezing through school. Giftedness has a much deeper and broader scope of talents, traits, and strengths than just how well a child performs in school. Some of the world's most well-known successes—Steve Jobs, Elizabeth Holmes, Mark Zuckerburg, Bill Gates, Russell Simmons, Albert Einstein, Oprah Winfrey, Walt Disney, Coco Chanel, Miguel Adrove, and Richard Branson—dropped out of school.[2] One might think that traditional school might actually hinder a gifted child destined for success.

How likely would even the most experienced teacher be to recognize the class clown with his uncanny sense of humor as being gifted? Or would a teacher see the above-average intelligence in his student he calls his "Lego maniac," because he only focuses on building creations instead of his classwork? How many teachers would look past the dismal report card to see the unchallenged genius sitting in their classroom, bored and ready to give up?

Trust Yourself as Much as You Trust Your Child's Teacher

Your gut is telling you your child is likely gifted, but no one at your child's school has mentioned this to you. Or perhaps you know in your heart that your gifted child could be learning so much more in school—it is just too easy for her. How do you handle this? Like so many of us, I had a strong faith and trust in our public school system, and because no educator ever said to me, "Your son is likely gifted and we need to have him tested and identified," I never seriously considered that my sons could be gifted when they were in school. I have three intelligent, talented, and wonderfully creative, but very different, gifted sons, and for far too many years, I did not see or recognize the gifted traits in my older two sons, and this detracted considerably from their education. Simply, and much too naively, I understood giftedness to be an educational issue that was addressed solely by the school. The teacher did not say my child was potentially gifted, so to me, my child was not gifted. Plain and simple. But, when your instincts tell you that your child is gifted, or that he should be challenged at a much higher level, trust those instincts and address your concerns with your child's teacher.

How Can We Ensure Teachers *Get Gifted?*

As a teacher, my beliefs about giftedness were in-line with the over-arching beliefs of most teachers: children who are gifted are high-achievers and excel in school. Lack of real data and information on giftedness in children provided to pre-service teachers is a widespread issue in teacher education programs and many gifted advocates are pushing for better teacher training on giftedness in children.

What is the solution to making sure all teachers *get gifted?* Training. Teachers should be thoroughly trained to understand the unique educational, social, and emotional needs of gifted children. Training should focus on dispelling the myths and misunderstandings about giftedness. Teachers should learn how to recognize in their gifted students the traits that can prevent a gifted student from succeeding, and the characteristics and behavioral traits of gifted children. Training teachers to understand giftedness is an ideal way for cash-strapped school districts with little to no gifted programming to begin implementing much-needed acceleration and differentiation in the classroom. With concise, effective training, we can increase understanding of gifted children, dispel the myths about giftedness, and all teachers can then *get gifted.*

Chapter 5

Traditional Schools and How They Miseducate Our Gifted Children

Traditional Schools: Not All Good & Not All Bad

Any government-operated, public system will always experience ups, downs, changes, criticisms, and praises. Such institutions' successes and failures ebb and flow, changing with the influential forces of the time. America's public school system is no different. Like any large institution, whether it is public or private, old or new, it is never all wrong or totally ineffective. Some teachers, schools, school systems, and states do a better job of educating our children than others depending on state and local school system laws, mandates, directives, expectations, and funding. Private schools often follow the lead of their public school counterparts, although they may have more freedom to make changes in the way they educate. By and large, private and public schools generally all teach in the same traditional educational methods we all know.

Traditional Schools Need a Transformation

Today, our public school system is under fire, and generating much criticism from many differing interests because it is failing on many levels to educate and prepare students for the requirements of our 21st century. Harold Sirkin, in his article, "To Fix U.S. Public Education, Take a Lesson From Countries That Top Student

Rankings," had this to say regarding America's performance in the latest round of international student testing:

> *First, they confirm what we already know: A lot of American schools are failing America's children—failing to teach them the basics, failing to prepare them to use the basics in the "real world," and failing to encourage them to aim for the top.*[1]

Many are calling for an educational transformation, not just a reformation, as the organizational structure of typical classrooms reflects the needs of long-gone historical trends. The change needs to be unlike any other school transfiguration and is needed more critically now than ever before. Our educational system needs to take a distinctly different and revolutionary path if it is to remain viable, if it is to serve all of our students well enough to successfully compete in our global market. Our current schools struggle to produce students with relevant real-world skills needed to meet future demands. "Today our collective vision for education is broader, our nation is more complex and diverse, and our technical capabilities are more powerful. But we continue to assume the factory-model classroom and its rigid bell schedules, credit requirements, age-based grade levels, and physical specifications when we talk about school reform," says Joel Rose in "How to Break Free of Our 19th-Century Factory-Model Education System."[2] Our world has changed enormously since the birth of our current, industrial-type educational system, yet schools have not evolved to meet the new challenges and requirements of our world's present-day demands.

Traditional Schools and the Neglect of Gifted Children: Federal Educational Initiatives

Of all the drastic changes necessary in our traditional school systems, one critical aspect must be addressed: the miseducation and neglect of our gifted students. In recent decades, we have seen our governments, federal and state, implement educational initiatives that have wreaked havoc on our educational system as a whole. The negative educational results have made their rounds in numerous national articles and op-ed pieces. We need to change our path to learning and reverse the damage to our education system—the schools, the teachers, and the students.

One such federal initiative which has spawned major educational problems in its wake is No Child Left Behind (NCLB). This Act, proposed by President George W. Bush and passed by the U.S. Congress in 2001, was a standards-based education reform based on the premise that educational outcomes can be improved by establishing measurable goals and setting high standards, goals and standards measured by standardized assessments which measured basic skills. Each state was responsible for implementing these standards and goals and for administering the standardized assessments in order to receive federal school funding which was tied to test score results. Some in education believe that the educational progress never materialized. "In fact, our classrooms are making even less progress towards improving overall educational performance and narrowing racial test score gaps than before NCLB became law," says Lisa Guisbond in her *Huffington Post* article, "NCLB Crashed and Burned—When Will We Ever Learn?"[3] NCLB significantly increased standardized testing in American public schools, while tying test scores to school and teacher performance evaluations. A decade of NCLB has most definitely left many of our children way behind—or completely left out.

Currently, one of the strongest push-backs from parents of school-age children comes from the overuse and misuse of standardized testing. As Cindy Long stated in her *NEA Today*, "Fears of low test scores and NCLB sanctions fueled the testing explosion."[4] Standardized testing became the elephant in the classroom when its presence grew into the prime educational focus which had everyone in the education industry hypnotized with bubbling in answer sheets. Continuing with the standardized testing trend amplified by NCLB were private, for-profit companies clamoring to jump on the profitable, standardized-testing band wagon. Standardized testing and all of its preparatory materials and prerequisite curriculum has created a lucrative cookie jar full of money-making opportunities, and many educational publishers and suppliers want to capitalize on this testing trend. This massive educational *faux pas* has diverted our nation's educational focus away from educating our children and on making sure our students do well on the standardized tests.

Despite all of its drawbacks, NCLB has seen some success with helping the below-average performers gain ground and show good educational progress despite its unfortunate legacy of the over-reliance on standardized testing. And yet, NCLB did leave some children behind—our gifted learners—approximately the top 2% of our students based on IQ scores. In fact, a 2008 report found that the controversial No Child Left Behind Act of 2001 indeed helped low-achieving students rise to meet a more rigorous course load, but shifted teachers' sights away from the gifted kids, who seemed capable of helping themselves stay on track.[5]

While schools were forced to focus on making sure the underperforming students caught up to proficiency standards, our gifted children were left to languish in classrooms, repeatedly being presented information they already knew. Although the vast majority of gifted children were likely at or above the required proficiency scores which schools and teachers needed to reach in order to not be penalized, gifted children were making considerably less yearly progress educationally than they should or could have had they been provided an appropriate education.

Now, we have another federal initiative, Race to the Top (RttT), which also does nothing to address the unique learning needs of our gifted children, and although the National Association for Gifted Children (NAGC) "requested that high ability children be included in specific parts of the application" and "an emphasis on closing the achievement gap between the highest performing disadvantaged students and their more advantaged peers . . . the Obama Administration totally ignored all suggestions and requests. RttT only provides support for the under-achieving student population."[6] So, once again, we have our gifted children underserved and unchallenged. It suffices to say that the education our gifted children have been provided in the last few decades has been inadequate which has caused several undesired, irreversible, and, in some cases, tragic results such as underachievement, higher dropout rates among gifted students, depression, and suicide. The rapidly growing number of gifted students turning to homeschooling demonstrates clearly that our gifted children have been significantly underserved in our traditional schools from more than a decade of the counterproductive federal educational initiatives which have snubbed them.

Gifted Children Need Gifted Education

I feel it bears repeating, gifted children *require* a challenging and appropriate education which meets their unique educational, social, and emotional needs and attends to their specific learning styles and level of achievement. If you take a look at the IQ (intelligence quotient) bell curve, the children at either end of the range of IQ distribution and at equal distances from the norm must understandably need a differentiated education to meet their inherent educational needs. Gifted children require a differentiated education that meets their specific learning needs as much as children well below the norm. Gifted children are not merely smarter, as in simply being above average; they are so much above the norm, that the development of their brains—the way they think, perceive, feel, envision, rationalize, and learn—is considerably different from children in the normal range of intelligence. Put simply, the farther from the norm any child lies, regardless which side of the norm they fall, the more they will need specific differentiated educational methods to succeed. Sadly, our current traditional school systems have failed to address this need, and our gifted children continually fail to show adequate yearly progress and fail to reach their educational potential.

What is "Teaching to the Middle"?

Our school systems today, by and large, have classroom teachers aiming instruction to the achievement level of the approximate middle one-third of the students in any one classroom because it is the most expedient and cost-effective mode of delivering an education. Teaching to the middle involves very little differentiated instruction, and its use is reinforced by the need to make sure students do well on high-stakes testing. The reasoning here is that the top one-third of the students will do just fine on the standardized test, the bottom one-third may fail no matter how much effort is put forth to remediate, but the instructional focus on the middle one-third will strategically give schools more bang for their buck on standardized test results.[7] Logically, this leaves students in the bottom one-third and the top one-third with an unfitting education. Because differentiating instruction is time-consuming and almost impossible for a teacher who already has too many demands on his time, teaching to the middle is the most expedient way to teach most effectively. This widely-used educational approach leaves gifted students unchallenged and undereducated in an educational environment enveloped in the focus of standardized testing and reaching basic proficiency standards.

Also, with so much of the educational focus on standardized test scores, classroom teachers, who are unfortunately evaluated by the results of their students' test scores, work hard to get as many of their students as possible reaching the minimum standards set forth by federal and state requirements. Along with teaching to the middle, classroom teachers work to raise the test scores of the bottom one-third of their students to minimum proficiency standards. Strategically, teaching to the middle one-third and the bottom one-third maximizes the teachers time with the highest likelihood of scores sufficient for the teacher to receive a satisfactory evaluation and not run the risk of losing her job. Do you see where this leaves gifted students in traditional schools whose eyes are trained on teaching to the test?

Failing Our Gifted Children: The Race to the Middle

Given the directives from the federal educational initiatives which public school teachers need to address in their classrooms, focusing valuable class time on the students who can make or break the test score results in a class—lower one-third and middle one-third—is kind of a no-brainer, especially if one's job is in jeopardy. While true in the U.S. that our most recent national educational initiatives have been successful in helping lower performing students demonstrate good educational progress, but *then why is America dropping in our educational rankings worldwide?*

Educational movements such as NCLB and RttT primarily focus on bringing up the lower-performing students to basic proficiency standards. Thus, the lower-performers educationally progress upwards towards the norm while the higher-ability students sit unchallenged and may actually fall downward towards the norm because their educational needs are totally neglected. Many sadly call this *The Race to the Middle*. I have one colleague, a university professor, who jokingly calls it *The Race to the Bottom*. Why is this happening? Why are we idly watching our high-performing students continually fall farther away from the educational levels they have the potential to achieve?

Most people, and including many teaching professionals, view IQ or intelligence as a linear measure: the higher a child's IQ, the easier it is for him to succeed in the classroom and, therefore, the less educational attention he needs. This is a total untruth, scientifically disproved many times over. And yet, governments, school systems, and teaching professionals provide an education to our gifted students based on this proven fallacy, believing that our high-ability and gifted students are fine on their own, or maybe they just need a bit more busy work. Money, individualized attention, classroom time, and school accountability focus on our educational systems' most important educational goal: to raise below-average scores to proficiency standards. For those who have already achieved the basic proficiency standards, the focus adapts to help them progress just a bit more and improve their scores. For the high-ability and gifted students who are likely well-beyond the basic proficiency standards, the focus ignores them and their educational needs which then, over time, causes our gifted learners to lose ground.

As a former teacher, I can empathize with, but not condone, this educational trend. I can easily understand a busy, over-stressed teacher finding it impractical and inefficient to use his personal time and money to focus on the neglected gifted learners in his classroom whom he may feel are already advantaged because of their above-average intelligence. At the same time, his job depends solely on making sure the majority of his students in his classroom reach basic, grade-level proficiency standards which he assumes all of his gifted students have already reached. As a result, our gifted students stagnate in the regular classroom, bored, unchallenged, and not learning any new skills, while the teacher must focus on those who have not reached the basic, grade-level standards.

The Consequences of the Miseducation of Gifted Students

Every child deserves to learn something new every day, but this is not happening in our traditional classrooms with our current educational initiatives. And while our gifted students sit bored and unchallenged, negative consequences such as discipline problems, neglecting school work, acting out, depression, underachievement, risky behaviors, and suicidal thoughts begin to grow among them. Alas, not only are our gifted students not flourishing educationally as they should, they are falling into unwanted and distressing situations. Teaching professionals may not readily recognize these educational, social, and emotional situations, as they may not understand all the facets of giftedness. Parents are usually the first to notice their gifted child exhibiting these difficult, painful, and tragic behaviors. When schools do nothing to respond to parents' concerns about their gifted children, parents begin to seek other educational options.

Gifted children's languishing in regular classrooms and the schools' failure to respond appropriately to the needs of these gifted children has lead to the ever-growing move to homeschooling among these families. Homeschooling has, without a doubt, proven to be an outstanding educational choice for gifted students. While misguided national educational movements, acts, and bills focus on raising test scores and improving America's ranking worldwide, our gifted children, who are capable of the sought-after high test scores, leave for the greener grasses of homeschooling, and they are taking their coveted high test scores with them.

Again, why are our overall standardized test scores not showing the desired improvement? Why is America dropping in our educational rankings worldwide? Do you think it may be because we are not focusing on those students who have the potential to improve our international education rankings with much-higher-than-average test scores? I do. I most definitely do. And this is why I homeschool.

Chapter 6

Stepping Off the Traditional School Roller Coaster

When to Give Up the Fight

If you are like me, you don't want to throw in the towel without a fight. Being the parents of gifted children, most of us have had to fight someone, somewhere to make sure our gifted child was receiving the education and attention he needed and deserved. But sometimes you have to throw in the towel and leave the traditional school behind. It is a difficult and emotional decision. Leaving a school you placed so much hope and trust in, believing it would provide the best education for your gifted child, can be heartbreaking and maddening. Now the roller coaster has truly sent you plummeting.

My family's roller coaster ride plummeted unexpectedly and very painfully with the last traditional school my youngest gifted son attended. It was the school we wholeheartedly believed to be the perfect school, the school we had bragged about to all who would listen, the school that had embraced our son just a year previously—and it had suddenly and inexplicably morphed into the most injurious, the most misinformed, and definitely the most unprofessional school we had ever endured. We just weren't prepared. We had been blindsided and were left hanging upside down on the roller coaster's traditional school loop-de-loop. Sheila Gingras, from Ottawa, Ontario, a mother of a highly gifted teenage daughter who had to leave her traditional school because of miseducation and negligence told me recently, "If I could turn back the clock, I would have trusted myself more and the schools less because years later I realized how different things could have been and how much happier our child's life, and our family's life, could have been." Her sentiments ring true for many parents of gifted children who realized it was time to throw in the towel and remove their gifted children from traditional school.

When my own family threw in the towel after it was clear our efforts to advocate for our youngest gifted son were useless, we sadly and quietly withdrew our son with just two months to go in his eighth grade year—two months before his eighth grade graduation, two months before the yearbook signing parties, two months before the end-of-school celebrations. With incredibly heavy hearts and battered emotions, we took our son away from the traditional school system which ignored his educational needs and we brought him home to heal and engage in an enriched educational environment which was perfectly attuned to his learning needs—homeschooling.

Gifted Students and Homeschooling

Our current educational system has under-served our gifted students for years, neglecting their unique learning needs and thwarting their ability to reach their full potential. "Gifted children are likely to be the next generation's innovators and leaders—yet the exceptionally smart are often invisible in the classroom, lacking the curricula, teacher input and external motivation to reach full potential," says Joan Brasher in her article, "Are gifted children getting lost in the shuffle?"[1]

Parents are tired of having to advocate for their gifted child and battle school systems, schools, and educators just to get an appropriate education for their gifted children. Despite the multitude of sources such as educational research studies, psychological research studies, professional educational and psychological articles, and historical data and statistics, our school systems still cling to the misguided notion that gifted education is expendable, not essential, and gifted students can thrive educationally without gifted programs. The distressing consequences from our school systems not providing the appropriate education our gifted students require are nothing less than neglect. We are *neglecting* the needs of these children. Although no direct statistics show the move by gifted students from traditional school to homeschool, significant anecdotal evidence shows that gifted students likely make up the single largest student population recently turning to homeschooling, and for understandable reasons.

As the saying goes, I've seen the writing on the wall or, for me, it is the writing on my website, www.crushingtallpoppies.com, in the form of hundreds of readers' comments and the many comments on my website's associated social media sites. My reader's comments relay, over and over, similar stories about their painful struggles when trying to get an appropriately challenging education for their gifted child within traditional schools.

> *Sadly, you've pretty much described our situation. We had to leave our family and move towns just to get an education for our son.*

> *When we approached them about our gifted child, we were told by the principal and district that they didn't have a gifted program because the whole district was set up for gifted kids.*

> *I have been left behind and damaged by traditional thinking and schooling and I hated every second of my school years right up until graduating high school. With the exception of the one or two teachers who "got it," it was a miserable time for me.*

> *I don't think he is getting the help he needs at school but I find myself talking to "professionals" that think he should be a genius since he's gifted and have no trouble flying through the standardized requirements. I keep praying for this to get easier.*

> *I can't tell you how many teacher conferences and meetings with the principal (ahem) we've endured—and how frequently we (the parents) have to educate the professionals about giftedness.*

> *I read your list and started to cry. I have been struggling with our school system to help our 2e daughter. The director of the "gifted" program asked me why my daughter couldn't get "all 4s" for grades if she was truly gifted.*

Although the details differed for each story, the plot was always much the same: *a gifted child was not receiving the education he needed; he began to show signs and symptoms such as underachievement, boredom, disengagement from school, and disruptive behavior because he was not being challenged appropriately in school; his parents' repeated attempts to get the school to provide an appropriate gifted education failed and so the parents turned to homeschooling to provide their gifted child the education he needed.* So many families riding on the same big, scary roller coaster ride. But now the families who are tired of the absurd fights with inflexible traditional schools can step onto an exciting and joyful ride once they begin homeschooling.

Homeschooling and gifted children are a perfect educational combination. A gifted child's intellectual development, thinking processes, and cognitive functions are very different from the neurotypical child, and thus these children take in information differently and more intensely than other children.[2] They often learn and think more deeply and quickly, and homeschooling can provide the necessary opportunities for a gifted child to thrive in an educational environment that meets her learning needs. The rich multitude of homeschooling resources and exceptional opportunities work together to form an optimal education easily tailored to fit the learning needs of gifted children and, really, the learning needs of all children.

Taking the Plunge: Braving the Homeschooling Waters

Although my first experience with homeschooling began out of necessity, I quickly fell in love with the incomparable freedom to design for my child a superior education that precisely fit his learning needs using the infinite variety of rich resources available. As we ventured through our homeschooling day, the little revelations of how fruitful homeschooling was astounded me, which furthered my love affair. Hands-on learning, first-hand experiences, spontaneous learning experiences, flexibility with school schedules, learning on weekends, freedom for educational travel (any trip can be a learning experience), fewer sick days (because you can still learn in your jammies, even if a bit under the weather), all made for the richest, most advantageous education possible. I came to understand fully that wonderful homeschool saying, *the world is my classroom.*

First Things First: The Infamous *Socialization* Question

Every homeschooler has heard, *What about socialization?* This quintessential question derives from the misinformed assumption that homeschooled children stay at home, isolated from other children their age. In reality, *homeschooling* is a misnomer of major proportion. Homeschoolers are far less cloistered than the traditionally-schooled children who sit in classrooms with only same-aged peers for six hours a day, five days a week. Homeschoolers have coined phrases such as car-schooling, world-schooling, and roam-schooling. *Schooling* is sitting within the brick-and-mortar walls of a traditional school, whereas homeschooling is learning everywhere. Homeschoolers, far from isolated, learn so much beyond those brick-and-mortar walls.

Socialization means "the learning of social skills, to operate successfully within one's society," which can happen anywhere, anytime, and with any-age person or persons. The explosive growth of homeschooling has made it so mainstream that homeschoolers now have innumerable opportunities available: classes at co-ops, playgroups, volunteer opportunities, field trips with other homeschoolers—all with a variety of people of all ages. *This* is real-world socializing—the way adults socialize in a multitude of situations with people of all ages at any time. Why do we believe that a tightly-run classroom full of same-age children where the number one rule is *no talking* is a place for children to learn social skills? Where children eat lunch in 20 minutes, again with *no talking?* Where recess has become almost non-existent, or can been taken away as punishment for *too much talking?* Traditional school sure doesn't seem to have the market cornered on the optimal place for children to learn good social skills that will benefit them in the real world.

Numerous Homeschooling Opportunities

An internet search of the word "homeschool" reveals the enormity of this burgeoning educational institution. National organizations; worldwide businesses; global, national, state, and local clubs and teams; enumerable curriculum retailers; co-ops; online schools and classes—the list seems endless. Homeschooling is big business because homeschooling is a huge educational reality.

Homeschoolers go on group field trips with children of all ages, learn in lively co-ops, take advantage of various volunteer opportunities, attend multi-age classes offered by various civic and private businesses such as museums, art supply stores, or sports events centers, and attend regular park days or game days. And when they come home after a busy, adventure-filled day full of all sorts of learning experiences, homeschoolers still have the opportunity to play with neighborhood children. Homeschoolers—a world full of learning is theirs for the taking! So what is holding you back?

I Can't Homeschool Because . . .

Doesn't homeschooling seem perfect? Well, it almost is, but just like anything else in this world, you must consider all sides, like homeschooling's time-commitment, the potential cost of curriculum and classes, and the need to plan, be organized, and become confident in your ability to educate your children. Which brings me around to that often-heard statement: *I can't homeschool because*

- I am not a certified teacher.

- I would go crazy being with my kids all day.

- I don't have a college education.

- I don't have enough money.

- I work.

- I need my "me" time.

We all have our own reasons. Pamela Price, author of the book, *How to Work and Homeschool*,[3] has this to say about making the decision to homeschool when you have doubts, especially if you work:

> *At first the very idea of working while homeschooling may seem like an impossible mission. After all, we all grew up believing that parents and kids spent their days apart and that interaction with one another should only ever center around dinner, homework, weekends, and summer. But if you do a little digging like I did, you soon discover that there is a dizzying array of options for reintegrating our lives. Best of all, the rewards of doing so extend far beyond the domain of education. With effort and thinking, one can create a more vibrant and satisfying work/live/play/learn experience than our parents or grandparents could imagine.*

You may find yourself at the point where you know homeschooling would be better for your gifted child, but fear you may not do it well or will fail to provide your child the education he needs. I have friends who have been homeschooling for years and they still worry if they are doing it right! The reality is, I have never really met a homeschooling family who has completely failed at homeschooling. In my fourteen years of homeschooling in three different states and in two different countries, I have never seen anyone truly fail at educating their child. On the other hand, I have seen three separate schools fail my youngest son. I have seen traditional schools fail many gifted children. In the introduction to their 2004 book, *Genius Denied*, Bob and Jan Davidson said,

> *Over the years, we have discovered that when it comes to leaving no child behind, highly gifted students are the most likely to fall through the cracks in American classrooms. They are the most likely to underachieve, to suffer the greatest gap between their potential and what is asked of them. This is what we mean by "genius denied."*[4]

Taking into account my experience and the data available, homeschooling has the much better track record for providing a good, sound education for any child. All the reasons why someone feels they may not be able to homeschool, or feel they may not succeed, can usually all be overcome. All you need to homeschool successfully is to love your child and sincerely want her or him to have the best education possible. It really is that simple.

Homeschooling Builds Strong Relationships

Okay, so I will admit, I am biased towards homeschooling. My husband and I have never regretted this life choice. Homeschooling has not only provided an outstanding education for our children, but it has also enriched and strengthened our family. If I had to give the one most important benefit of homeschooling for my family, it would have to be the deepening and strengthening of my relationships with all three of my sons. In fact, to "enhance family relationships between children and parents and among siblings" is one of the most common reasons given for homeschooling according to Brian D. Ray, Ph.D., in his article, "Research Facts on Homeschooling," from the National Home Education Research Institute.[5]

I know without doubt that I would not have had the extraordinarily close, loving and respectful relationships with any of my three sons if I had not had the extra quality time with them, day in and day out, which homeschooling afforded us. Homeschooling brought us closer and formed strong bonds between each member of my family. Strong relationships with your children can be key in providing your children the wisdom to steer clear of life's unfortunate temptations, and give them the backbone to make wise choices. Homeschooling educates, but more important, it forms stronger, more loving bonds with your children, and within your family.

Chapter 7

Sharing the Homeschool Love: Resources, Scheduling, Teaching

I am convinced that homeschooling can deliver a rich and highly-experiential education. I've homeschooled in three different states and one province, and each place legislated homeschooling differently. Some were hands-off while offering very little help or resources for homeschooling families. Some required more contact and reporting from homeschoolers, but offered many resources, groups, and support. If you are just about to step off the big, scary roller coaster into homeschooling, look into all the laws, regulations, resources, and support for your area. Simply enter "homeschool" and your state or province into a search engine, and you'll find organizations which will help you navigate the local terrain. GHF also maintains a list of local contacts who can help you find resources and support specific to the needs of gifted and 2e families (http://giftedhomeschoolers.org/resources/local-support/).

Homeschooling Your Gifted Child

Gifted students, and especially twice-exceptional gifted students, have unique educational needs that are addressed effectively with homeschooling. Again, traditional school classrooms are organized to teach a group of twenty or more students: differentiating and modifying the curriculum to meet every student's educational ability level and learning need is difficult, if not impossible. Thus, teachers naturally have to guide the learning outcomes and the educational goals towards the average ability level of the class. Differentiation is a hallmark of homeschooling. Homeschooling has the unique potential to reach and teach every student using a tremendous variety of learning resources and experiences perfectly tailored to fit a gifted child's ability level, interests, and learning style. As much as the traditional classroom is one-size-fits-all, homeschooling is one-size-fits-one. When homeschooled, gifted students will blossom because their educational needs are being perfectly met using the richest of resources.

The gift of hindsight. Oh yeah, I would have most definitely educated my three gifted sons differently. First, I would have valued the unparalleled education homeschooling offers much more than I did when I first began homeschooling, and I would have capitalized more on the rich variety of learning experiences only homeschooling can offer in my initial years of homeschooling. Second, I would have questioned traditional schools' ability to provide a quality education much more than I did. As a former public school teacher, I believed that our traditional school systems knew the education of all children better than anyone, and that they were nearly infallible when it came to educating my children. Valuing homeschooling more and trusting traditional schools less would have provided my children a significantly higher quality of education, a more effective and efficient educational path, a greater opportunity to develop their self-confidence, and the freedom to be themselves. It would have also minimized my children's experiences with bullying, being judged by stringent grading systems, being left out, and exposure to behaviors such as drugs, alcohol, and violence. With the ever-growing popularity of homeschooling,[1] homeschooling's educational opportunities are nearly limitless.

Homeschooling is Going Mainstream

As homeschooling rapidly grows in popularity, this educational trend yields ever more resources, groups, co-ops, classes, and opportunities for homeschoolers. What good news for those of you about jump into homeschooling! Homeschooling is becoming mainstream—accepted and respected. The major growth in homeschooling and the wealth of educational resources are also good news for gifted and 2e students who require a broad range of learning experiences and challenges to meet their unique learning needs.

When I first jumped into the unconventional educational waters of homeschooling fifteen years ago, resources were limited. Few businesses catered to homeschoolers looking for curriculum and educational materials. Only at this point, the beginning of my years of homeschooling, did my experience as a classroom teacher help me procure an assortment of educational resources for my son. My years of teaching at an underprivileged inner-city school, where money for classroom supplies was nonexistent, greatly honed my skills for creatively finding or making much-needed educational materials. I shopped the sales at the educational materials stores. I was a regular on ebay looking for used textbooks and teacher's manuals. I scoured the internet for educational websites and software. I became a highly-skilled educational materials sleuth. But that was then. Fifteen years later, homeschooling families have more varied and exceptional resources and opportunities than they could ever use. The tremendous variety of exceptional homeschooling resources so readily available is certainly a big plus for homeschoolers, but it can also be a huge temptation!

Falling Into Temptation

"I bought too many books. It just all looked so great!" I often hear this sentiment from fellow homeschoolers and am very much guilty of this, as my Amazon.com account can attest. The richness and educational value of homeschooling resources makes typical public school materials pale in comparison. From free Ivy League courses online, to exceptional curriculum choices like a program that uses music to teach science concepts, to a multitude of educational apps, software, and websites—I get so amped up just thinking about all the exquisite educational resource options that are available. And if you fall victim to overbuying homeschool materials, no worries, you can always resell it at local homeschool fairs or on online homeschool buy-and-sell groups (see *Resources Appendix*).

I just love utilizing the wonderful and exciting learning materials not usually found in traditional schools. I find the depth and breadth of homeschooling resources more exciting than eating chocolate or buying new shoes. And then to be able to use these resources to provide my child with an unparalleled, rich, and varied educational experience? How exhilarating! I also love using these resources myself, learning right along with my sons. Yes, I have a wild and exciting love affair with homeschooling.

Homeschooling and Gifted Go Together like a Horse and Carriage

Are you now convinced that there are enough homeschooling resources out there to satiate your gifted child's voracious appetite for knowledge and educational challenge? Would you agree that it would also be excitingly easy to find just the right materials for your twice-exceptional gifted child? Also, you do understand that you don't need to reproduce the often-times mediocre educational delivery system of traditional classrooms which likely underserved your gifted child, right? With the wide variety and different delivery methods of homeschool educational resources (books, apps, software, websites, and local and online classes) available to homeschoolers, you will be able to find the right educational fit for you twice-exceptional and gifted child. Plus, you may find that you don't need to spend your day teaching if your child finds an engaging online physics class or a fun iPad math app that encourages independent learning. Your gifted child will have the unique opportunity to participate in independent learning which is an excellent way to nurture a lifelong learner. The advantages of homeschooling your gifted child keep multiplying!

Sorting Through All the Exquisite Resources

The one downside to the plentitude of all of these wonderful homeschool resources, besides buying too much, is sorting through them to find the right fit for your gifted child. Gifted parent forums can be highly informative places where you can chat with and ask questions of other parents who are also homeschooling their gifted children. The knowledgeable experience of others can greatly benefit you here. Learning from other parents' experiences with specific programs and resources, and getting recommendations from other parents, is undeniably helpful when navigating the plethora of educationally-rich resources. Whether you are looking for the best math curriculum for your visual-spatial gifted daughter, or trying to find an engaging Latin program for your gifted ADHD third grader who learns with short but loaded bursts of information, online parent forums can provide a wealth of parental experience, solutions, advice, and recommendations for you when trying to find that just-right class or curriculum.

Finding the Best-for-Your-Gifted-Child Resources

Choices in educational materials and resources should be based on your child's needs and your family's needs. What works extremely well for one child may end up being a huge disappointment for another. This is unavoidable and it happens to all of us. When this happened to me, I tried to look at it another way: if your child were in a traditional school, she would not have an alternative—every child must use the same state-adopted textbooks. Your child would have to learn from curriculum choices made by someone far-removed from the classroom who doesn't know your child or her educational needs. But, with homeschooling, you do have a choice in resources and educational materials, and some of those choices may not pan out. Don't feel like you have to use it just because you bought it. As I mentioned before, you can likely sell it. Of course, the online classes you paid for, only to discover that they bore your child, cannot be sold, but subscriptions to educational websites most often can be canceled. The advice here, and yes, I have been guilty of this also, is to not force yourself to use it if it is not working for your child. Again, I suggest researching and getting recommendations for online resources from gifted parenting forums or websites (see *Resources Appendix*).

When purchasing homeschool materials:

1. Look to gifted parenting forums and websites and to other gifted homeschoolers for help and advice on resources and materials before you buy. Ask lots of questions.

2. Homeschooling books, materials, and other resources can be sold when you no longer need them.

3. If a program, resource, or curriculum which you purchased does not work for your child, don't feel the need to use it just because you bought it. You can buy and sell used homeschooling materials through many different venues.

What Time? How Much Time? When?

Once you have decided on the best-fit educational resources for your gifted child, the learning begins. Do not try to reproduce a typical classroom schedule like those in a brick-and-mortar school. If your gifted teen likes to sleep in and works best starting school work at 10:00 a.m., then by all means provide her that optimal learning schedule. If your gifted first grader is an early riser and can't wait to conduct a week's worth of science experiments in the kitchen at 5:00 a.m., do what you can to accommodate him. Teaching your child at opportune times leads to those serendipitous teachable moments which make for the most permanent learning.

Accelerating Your Gifted Child

Books in hand, online classes reserved, flexible schedule penciled in—now the teaching begins.

Looking back on all of my homeschooling experiences, I wish I would have been more confident in accelerating my three children. For gifted students who grasp information and concepts quickly and require less repetition to master a skill or concept, moving at their own pace is vital, even if this means skipping over lessons, chapters, or even grade levels. This is where my teacher training and years in the classroom hindered how I homeschooled. I was so conditioned to think that each lesson had to be mastered before the next lesson could be taught, that each box had to be ticked before we could move on. I was wrong, oh so wrong. If and when my gifted sons showed eagerness to move beyond what we were learning at the time, I should have heeded their need to skip ahead.

It was my youngest son's wise-beyond-her-years piano teacher who taught me this lesson. When my son expressed his desire to play a particular difficult piece far above his level, instead of saying, "No, you have to learn these prerequisite piano skills before you can play that piece," she went ahead and let him tackle the challenging piece. To my amazement, he attacked that piece like a champ and didn't stop until he got it. I realized then that some gifted children learn by taking one step after another and some, like my son, just leap to the top step right away, learning what was missed on the lower steps while standing on that high vantage point. This experience also showed me how gifted children can falter with the easiest assignments, but soar at the most challenging. But wait, what about the *gaps* they may have from skipping or accelerating?

Filling in the Gaps

Way back when I was student teaching a fourth grade class, the school's policy was that if a third grade student had not memorized the multiplication facts, he or she was not allowed to move on to fourth grade. In the fourth grade class in which I was student teaching, one student had been an exception to this rule because she had done well in all other subjects. I was assigned to tutor and drill her on her multiplication facts while the rest of the class was learning 2- and 3-digit multiplication. As we sat in the back of the class, I noticed something phenomenal. This student, who struggled to memorize her multiplication facts—as assessed on a timed test—was able to keep one ear on me while paying attention to the instruction being given by the teacher on solving the multi-digit multiplication problems. I decided to informally give her some of the multiplication problems the rest of the class was working on. She nailed them all! Forcing her to sit through the grueling drill-and-kill to memorize those multiplication facts was holding her back. So what if she couldn't spit out her multiplication facts at the speed of sound? She was able to successfully understand and solve the higher level multiplication problems without having to pass those nasty timed multiplication facts tests first. She easily mastered multi-digit multiplication. And wasn't that the goal, after all?

None of us can know *everything*, and some of us have gone on to attain higher education degrees despite not having memorized all of our multiplication facts or knowing how to be good spellers or having memorized all the state capitals. Those "gaps" are only important if your child is struggling with understanding new material without grasping the underlying the skills or concepts. If the new material is something your child is passionate about, like my son's very technical piano piece or my student's desire to learn 2- and 3-digit multiplication, your child will most likely fill in those gaps easily and incidentally as he happily tackles the more challenging material.

Teach Outside The Box & Think Outside The Book

Teach Outside the Box

As a homeschooler, you do not need to purchase and use a boxed curriculum which may lock you in a method of teaching, having to tick off all of the boxes before moving on. Gifted children seem to want to learn sometimes by flittering, sometimes by flying, and then sometimes by soaring. Don't box them in.

Think Outside the Book

Our world, our universe offers us so much to learn, see, hear, feel, and experience. Homeschooling offers the unique opportunity, unshared by traditional school students, to expose your gifted child to the world—a world beyond what is in a textbook. Let your gifted child learn, see, hear, feel, and experience his world in real life, outside of a book. *The best learning experiences exist outside of a textbook.*

Four Essential Homeschool Lessons

Homeschool Lesson #1: *You do not need to be a certified classroom teacher to successfully homeschool.*

Teachers have been trained to utilize educational methods and teaching strategies that most efficiently and productively educate a group, a class of twenty or so students. These methods and strategies, while imparting knowledge, skills, and information, must also aid the teacher in maintaining discipline and organization in a classroom setting, and are not necessarily the most optimal way to educate a child, especially a gifted child. Without the constraints of having to maintain discipline, strict organization, and accountability to school systems and parents, your options of educational methods, teaching strategies, and even the curriculum you choose to use in your homeschool are nearly infinite.

Homeschool Lesson #2: *You do not need to use boxed curriculum or traditional textbooks, workbooks, and tests to successfully homeschool.*

If you use them at all, use pre-packaged resources as basic outlines to guide you in what skills and concepts your child should be learning. The sky is the limit for homeschool resources, methods, and strategies, so do not limit yourself to just the traditional textbooks, workbooks, and tests. Traditional resources are developed for classrooms, accountability, and teaching to a group of same-age students. Learning can come from many sources, not just books. As infants and toddlers, our children learned some major developmental skills like walking and talking without the help of textbooks, didn't they? And many gifted children learned to read, on their own, without a textbook.

Homeschooling affords you the most effective and beneficial of teaching methods: first-hand, hands-on, real-life learning. Like a true homeschooler, I learned this while homeschooling with my middle son in his sixth grade year. We were happily immersed in a physical science unit, learning about simple machines. At one point, my son just could not grasp some of the concepts of inclined planes despite our many attempts at rereading, drawing, and reviewing. Frustrated and at my wit's end, and almost as a form of punishment for making this awesomely fun science lesson hit a disappointing snag, I sent my 12-year-old son outside to build his own inclined planes. He knew where the scrap wood and tools were so he went outside to start his project, and I was relieved to have a few moments to unclench my teeth and to reassure myself that I did not make a grave error by choosing to homeschool. During the hour that I sat, mustering up all my teacher training in order to magically produce the perfect teaching strategy to help my son understand the forces that work on inclined planes, my 12-year-old son had not only unraveled the mystery of the forces that act on inclined planes for himself, but he taught me a crucial homeschooling lesson: learning does not need to come from textbooks. In fact, the best way to learn may not be from books at all.

As I walked outside, my eyes fell on two huge inclined planes constructed from every bit of the scrap wood from the garage. One inclined plane was shorter with a steeper slope and the other was a longer inclined plane with a more gradual slope. And my son proudly demonstrated each and every inclined plane concept he had previously struggled to understand on paper. Duh! Why hadn't I realized before now that this was the best way to learn most anything? I was a kindergarten teacher, and kindergarten is all about first-hand, hands-on learning. But then again, one can only imagine what chaos would ensue if a middle school teacher sent her entire class outside to use hammers, nails, and wood to master the concepts of inclined planes. I admonished myself for not turning to hands-on learning sooner, but I didn't beat myself up for long because the sense of pride and elation my son was oozing from every pore of his body overtook me. It was truly a revelation, and the one I credit with entirely changing the way I looked at homeschooling. The downside? What were we to do with those two huge inclined planes of sufficient size to double as a big rig auto mechanic's ramps?

Homeschool Lesson #3: *When it comes to learning resources, teach outside the box—the boxed curriculum.*

From that autumn morning, as I stood alternately staring between those two glorious inclined planes and my elated, beaming son, I knew our homeschooling had permanently changed for the better. The dry erase board stood unused the rest of our school year, and the dining room was no longer our classroom. We learned, we felt, we saw, we heard, and we experienced. And I mean *we* learned, not *he* learned and *I* taught. So, my son and I began to learn anywhere and everywhere. Field trips were daily events, the floor was a regular classroom desk, our van was our most useful homeschool resource, and our literature hour was spent every day at lunch at a park overlooking the St. Lawrence Seaway. I fell head-over-heels in love with homeschooling at that point, and learning became a family passion.

Homeschool Lesson #4: *You do not need to tick off all the boxes, take all the tests, and cover each and every lesson, chapter, and grade-level book.*

The teacher in me still rears her inconvenient, ugly head. I am a box-ticker. I derive extreme satisfaction from ticking off every box on my list, and this personality trait, as well as my teacher training, carried over into my homeschooling. Sadly, my most prized remnant of our early days of homeschooling is a math workbook that has *every* page, all the way to the very last one, totally completed. To me, this meant we were successful and accomplished. To my son, completing this workbook probably felt like he was being dragged through pure I-already-know-this monotony.

I learned the hard way, but you can benefit from my mistakes. Your child will not have gaps in her education if you skip a lesson you feel she already understands, or she skips a chapter she covered at the museum classes she took, and she will not miss out if you skip an entire grade level. Scary thoughts, for sure. When you insist on covering every page, every lesson, every chapter or every grade level just because it is there, you could be holding your gifted child back. To calm your anxiety and give you assurance that you are doing the right thing when skipping along, give your child a test beforehand. If it is a chapter you feel that can be skipped, give your child the end-of-chapter test before you skip. If she passes, she's got it. In traditional schools, this is called pretesting: test the child beforehand to determine if she has mastered the concepts you will be teaching so that you do not have to have her revisit something she already knows. So, pretest and skip along.

Enriching the Social Life of Your Gifted Child: Peers

What is life without friends? Children and adults alike need and want true and lasting friendships, but for the gifted child, finding a friend among his same-age classmates in his traditional school classroom to whom he can relate intellectually is quite difficult. Dividing students into grade levels by age understandably cause a gifted child who may be several grade levels ahead of his same-age classmates to have difficulty finding a true peer—one who gets the higher level of social interactions and discourse. "It is common knowledge that gifted children often prefer the company of adults or older children. The reason is obvious: They don't need to explain who they are or how they know what they know. Accepted as bright, competent individuals, the stigma of being smart is not a stigma at all," explains Dr. James Delisle in his book, *Parenting Gifted Kids*.[2]

My experience with gifted children and finding friendships is multifold—from remembering a classmate I grew up with from grade school through high school whose only social interaction at every recess was the words on the pages of a book she was reading, to recalling my years as a teacher and seemingly having at least one student each year in my class who was a loner, but loved engaging in lengthy conversations with me which made her light up, to experiences with my own gifted sons. And although there are no easy solutions, you can help your gifted child find true peers.

Groups, clubs, classes, and teams which focus on your gifted child's passions, strengths, and interests provide opportunities to meet like-minded peers with similar interests. Volunteer opportunities are also a rich resource which can further your child's interests, enrich his social and emotional development, and extend his learning. Enrolling your child in after-school, weekend, and summer gifted programs is another way to boost your child's social and emotional growth and provide an opportunity for your child to make strong friendships. All seem easy enough, and they do provide workable solutions, but be prepared to try a few before finding the one that works for your child.

I offer the caveat, *be prepared to try a few before finding the one that works for your child,* because I searched many options for my gifted sons to help them find strong, lasting friendships. We have moved many times and once we land in each new hometown, my priority is to find the right social opportunities for my gifted children. This has given me hard-earned experience in this realm and I have two bits of advice.

1. **Don't give up!** Be prepared for what can seem like a never-ending search with some opportunities not working out as hoped. With our last move, the opportunities for a good social environment for our gifted son were out there, but many did not turn out as we had hoped, so we had to continue our search. I kept reminding myself, as well as my gifted son, not to give up hope and to accept that it may take some time. I had to take many steps out of my comfort zone to continually email, call, and ask around to the point where I felt like a pest. But, our long search was finally fruitful. Our gifted son found a

highly-engaging robotics team with teammates and mentors who are all on the same page.

2. **If you can't find what you need, create your own.** I've had experience with this one, too. When my search for groups of like-minded kids didn't turn up much, I created my own group, the *North Alabama Parents of Gifted Children*. One morning, after a miserable night of tossing, turning, and worrying about my struggle to find a social environment for my gifted son to blossom in, I created a Facebook page for NAPGC hoping to gather other local parents of gifted children for socializing and support. Things just snowballed from there. Within a month of forming my Facebook page, I was asked to help form the *North Alabama Association for Gifted Children* in conjunction with the *Alabama Association for Gifted Children* and the *National Association for Gifted Children*. What I learned from this worthwhile and rewarding experience is, *if you build it, they will come*. The two groups became one and was full of families with one commonality: improving the lives of gifted children. In the end, my family truly received more than we had expected in the way of empathetic support, sharing of resources, and lasting friendships. So, go ahead and form your own group of teens who want to code, or girls who are interested in science, or families who love geocaching. You will be surprised by the many rewarding experiences!

Chapter 8

Education and the Future

Your Gifted Child's Future

No matter where you and your family are on your journey with your gifted child, we all look to our children's future. For some of us, we look with trepidation because of the struggles we have had raising a gifted child within society's misguided opinions of our gifted children—struggles we cannot speak about openly because of our fear of the negative reactions that inevitably occur—the eye rolling, the disbelief that raising a gifted child can be difficult, or the downright smug attitude that says, "Stop bragging about your gifted child!" It has been a long haul for so many of us who parent gifted and 2e children.

In some ways, we can make our gifted children's childhood less stressful and more rewarding by knowing and understanding more about giftedness. Perhaps from learning more about the burdens of giftedness, and maybe through our own children's first-hand experiences, we know that often times the most significant source of emotional, social, and educational stress for our gifted children is having to learn and socialize in a traditional school setting which does not understand them. It is often a painful, lonely situation for them considering that if they attend a school of approximately 400 students, there would likely only be seven other gifted children like themselves with whom they *may* find a connection. Armed with knowledge and experience, we can foresee and hopefully avert some of the painful situations our gifted children can find themselves in.

Protecting Your Gifted Child

A good parent knows that you can't shield your children from all bad experiences, nor should you. Adversity strengthens resilience, and resilience should be nurtured in all children. But certain situations require us to act to protect our gifted children. Bullying, trouble fitting in socially, disengagement in school, difficulty finding true peers can cause harmful emotional, social, and educational distress that lasts a lifetime, and so warrant immediate intervention and advocacy. If your child is in a traditional school setting, intervention and advocacy efforts are focused at the school level, often resulting in a difficult, unproductive fight that leaves parents feeling confused, hurt, and angry. This happens much more than it should. And this is when parents often take their gifted children in hand and step off that big, scary roller coaster to bring their child home to a better education.

Bringing Your Gifted Child Home to Heal and to Learn

I hope you have come to see the vibrant and rewarding way of life homeschooling is for educating gifted and 2e children. Homeschooling often helps to either ease or remedy the many specific educational, emotional, and social ills these children face when they feel forced to conform to the confines and social mores prevalent in traditional schools. Issues, such as bullying, not fitting in socially, and the disengagement from learning, often improve once gifted and 2e children are brought home for their education.

Bullying

Although bullying is prevalent across many age groups and throughout many social situations, we have all seen news media reports of the many incidences of serious bullying occurring most often at traditional schools where students are away from their parents and observant adults are far fewer than in other social situations. From my personal experience, the majority of homeschooling activities and classes are attended by the parents as well as the children; with so many watchful adult eyes, the incidence of unchecked schoolyard bullying is often reduced. Although bullying can occur anywhere at any time, the common social make-up of homeschool gatherings offers a less-than-optimal chance for it to occur.

Fitting In

Children feel a strong need to belong to a group of peers and fit in, but in the traditional school setting, gifted and 2e children often feel as though they don't fit in with their same-age peers. If your gifted child feels as though she does not fit in among her same-age peers at her traditional school, homeschooling and homeschooling groups may offer a more inclusive and accepting social environment. Homeschool events and activities are commonly attended by parents, children, and siblings forming a multi-age group with diverse abilities and interests. It is within inclusive gatherings like these that gifted children have a greater likelihood of finding a true intellectual peer than in a traditional, same-age, lock-step classroom. For the most part, homeschoolers commonly strive to focus on being inclusive while being very accepting of all differences, and homeschoolers rarely segregate themselves by strict age/grade levels for any sort of class or activity

Gifted Advocacy for All Gifted Children

Whether due to cultural, financial, socioeconomic, or racial reasons, some gifted children remain unidentified, misdiagnosed, underserved, or discriminated against and can flounder and fail in our brick-and-mortar schools. If they have no adult in their lives to advocate for their needs, they will continue to have the common struggles so many gifted children experience. As parents of gifted children, we must continue to advocate to improve the lives of *all* gifted children. Although we may be successfully homeschooling our own gifted child, or our gifted child is thriving in a traditional school setting, many gifted children remain neglected and underserved. Society and traditional schools disregard a significant student population with unique emotional, social, and educational needs. When these needs go unmet or ignored, gifted children are prevented from fulfilling their potential, robbing them of their future as successful and productive adults. Almost sounds like a crime, doesn't it?

Who loses when a gifted child's intellectual strengths are not only not nurtured, but totally neglected? Is society missing out on a brilliant neurosurgeon? Are we bypassing an earth-shattering discovery by a forward-thinking scientist? Are we losing the next creative engineer who can find the way to harness a new energy source? A great writer? A soul-touching artist? How can we sit back and watch a child have his or her future stolen by those with misguided opinions of or belief in the fallacies about giftedness?

Finding Your Advocacy Voice

After my youngest son experienced some of the worst emotional and social repercussions from teachers unaware of what giftedness is and what gifted characteristics and traits can look like in a the school setting, I turned to advocacy. The emotional pain my son suffered due to the neglect of his educational needs, the educators' inexperience with his classic gifted behaviors, and the inappropriate discipline by teachers because of those misidentified gifted behaviors, all helped me find my advocacy voice. No child should have to suffer simply because he was born gifted. I ask you to advocate, especially for those who do not have an advocates' voice. With our united voices— whether through blogging, joining in online conversations, participating in Twitter chats, public speaking, face-to-face conversations—we will improve the educational, social, and emotional futures of our gifted children everywhere.

Advocating for Gifted Education

We can first begin to advocate and work towards changing the long-held but completely erroneous beliefs of our educational system, which has long miseducated and underserved our gifted children. Too many teachers have little to no training on understanding gifted learners in an educational setting. With inadequate training, teachers will continue to follow the myth that "all gifted children are smart and excel in school." I know this. I once was one of those woefully misguided teachers, and I worry whether or not I overlooked or failed to identify a truly gifted student because she didn't exhibit the "gifted children are smart and excel in school" characteristics.

Regardless of whether your gifted child is homeschooled or thriving in a traditional school setting, your voice is needed to advocate for all gifted children. During my first interview for my first teaching position at an at-risk, inner city school, my principal imparted to me the wisest observation I have ever heard:

> *You may look at these children and see that their family lives are hopeless. You may feel that, as hard as you try, these kids may never utilize the education you work so hard to deliver to them. But you know what? These kids, education or not, will grow up to being voting citizens in our society. When they have the opportunity to vote and change my world, your world, our world, we will need them to vote intelligently. We need them to be productive members of society, or our society will not stand. That is why their education is important!*

And that is why advocating for all gifted children is important.

Advocating for the Best Education for All Children

Every child is our future, and our future depends on them. Advocating for the most appropriate education for every gifted child will benefit our future. Advocating for the best education for all children benefits the future of our world.

Chapter 9

If I Could Do It All Over Again

There are No Do-Overs

Traditional school is like taking a beautiful, sun-loving, tall poppy waiting to burst forth and bloom, and then placing a box over it, controlling what it needs to grow, and severely limiting its potential so that the poppy develops into a flower so unlike what it was meant to be, it's unrecognizable.

I have a dear friend with a beautiful mind who lives far away from me. I cherish our long, deep talks on the phone. Our conversations are spiritual, wise, and intellectually stimulating. We discuss politics, history, religions, cultures, and psychology, but most often we discuss parenting. She is a thoughtful, balanced, and exceptional mother. One day when discussing our children, she was relaying to me a small, concerning situation with one of her children. As she mused over how to handle it, she suddenly said something I found so profound, I will never forget t: "There are no do-overs in parenting."

But if I Did Have a Do-Over, I Would . . .

If I had a do-over, I would have homeschooled all three of my sons for all of their years in school, until college.

I would have homeschooled them to preserve their fresh and positive outlook on life, their innocence, and their naiveté until it was the right time to let them go.

I would have homeschooled them so that they would have never had an unnecessarily cruel taste of failure, of being bullied, or of unfairness.

I would have homeschooled them so they would never have suffered a loss of self-esteem or felt that they were somehow *less*.

I would have homeschooled them so that we could have shared so much more of our lives together: the special times, the happy times, the sad times, the educational times, and the fun times.

I would have homeschooled them so that they could truly be free to happily grow into the men they were born to be without the struggle of the artificial and unnatural constraints and parameters set by traditional schools.

I would have homeschooled them because that is the only way to have given them the best educational experiences possible.

Life can be cruel, it can be unfair, and our children learn resilience from failure. Yet life can be unnecessarily cruel with too many negative experiences, impeding the healthy emotional and social development of a child. Resilience may not be learned from too many negative experiences. I believe there is a point when your child is too close to the edge where too much failure can cause him to quit, and too many negative experiences can damage or simply break his spirit.

If I had a do-over, I would have homeschooled all three of my sons for all of their years in school to make sure they never got so close to that edge where I feared they would quit or their spirit would be mangled and broken.

If I had a do-over, I would have never allowed us to step on the big, scary roller coaster ride traditional school seems to send our gifted children on. And then I would have taught outside the box and thought outside the book.

Resources Appendix

Homeschool Curriculum Resale, Buy, Sell, and Swap

ebay: http://www.ebay.com
> Thousands of books, materials, and resources ideal for homeschooling.

eHomeschoolClassifieds http://homeschoolclassifieds.com
> One of the largest websites for buying and selling new and used homeschool materials.

GHF Amazon Store: http://astore.amazon.com/giftedhomesch-20
> Books, materials, and resources recommended by homeschooling and gifted/2e families. (A portion of every purchase goes to support GHF.)

The Swap: http://www.theswap.com
> Started in 1996, one of the oldest used curriculum site on the internet.

Vegsource: http://www.vegsource.com/homeschool/
> A popular homeschooling section with a used curriculum buy, sell or swap board.

Don't forget to check with your local homeschool groups and organizations for opportunities to buy, sell, or swap homeschool curriculum locally.

Gifted Parent Forums

Davidson Gifted Issues Discussion Forum
> http://giftedissues.davidsongifted.org/BB/

Gifted Homeschoolers Forum
> http://giftedhomeschoolers.org/resources/parent-resources/

Gifted Support Groups on Facebook

Gifted Homeschoolers Forum
> https://www.facebook.com/GiftedHomeschoolersForum

Gifted Underachievers
https://www.facebook.com/groups/giftedunderachievers/

Gifted Unschooling
https://www.facebook.com/groups/giftedunschooling/

Moms of Gifted Kids
https://www.facebook.com/groups/217894068300462/

Teacher Resource Books

Scholastic Teacher's Store: http://www.scholastic.com/teachers/
Homeschooling parents can create an account and purchase professional teaching materials from Scholastic's Teacher's Store.

Evan-Moor: http://www.evan-moor.com
Provides educators with practical, creative, and engaging PreK-8 materials to support and enrich the core curriculum.

Mailbox Magazines: http://www.theeducationcenter.com
Monthly magazines which offer many classroom activities that can be easily adapted to homeschooling. You can also find single copies at teacher supply stores or used on websites like ebay.

Articles, Research, and Information on Gifted Education

GHF Articles Page
http://giftedhomeschoolers.org/resources/parent-and-professional-resources/articles/

Crawford, Amy, "The poor neglected gifted child," *Boston Globe*, March 6, 2014. http://www.bostonglobe.com/ideas/2014/03/15/the-poor-neglected-gifted-child/rJpv8G4oeawWBBvXVtZyFM/story.html

Kell, Harrison J., David Lubinski, and Camilla P. Benbow, "Who Rises to the Top? Early Indicators," *Association for Psychological Studies*, Vanderbilt University, 2013.
https://my.vanderbilt.edu/smpy/files/2013/02/Kell-Lubinski-Benbow-20132.pdf

Wai, Jonathan, "Three Reasons Why Americans Ignore Gifted Children," *Psychology Today*, September 19, 2012.
http://www.psychologytoday.com/blog/finding-the-next-einstein/201209/three-reasons-why-americans-ignore-gifted-children

Visual-Spatial Learners

GHF Articles Page: Learning Styles and Preferences
http://giftedhomeschoolers.org/resources/parent-and-professional-resources/articles/learning-styles-preferences/

Visual-Spatial Resource: http://www.visualspatial.org
A sister organization of the Gifted Development Center
(http://www.gifteddevelopment.com/).

Sword, Lesley, "I think in pictures, you teach in words: The gifted visual-spatial learner," *Tall Poppies Magazine*, 2011.
http://www.giftedchildren.org.nz/national/article4.php
A wonderful article discussing identifying and supporting visual-spatial learners.

Gifted Underachievement

GHF Articles Page
Numerous articles covering gifted and 2e issues.
http://giftedhomeschoolers.org/resources/parent-and-professional-resources/articles/

"Considering Underachievement in Gifted Learners," The Grayson School, March 20, 2014.
http://thegraysonschool.org/considering-underachievement-gifted-learners-1356

Karnes, Ph.D., Frances, Kristen Stephens, Ph.D., and Sylvia Rimm, Ph.D., *When Gifted Students Underachieve: What You Can Do About It* (The Practical Strategies Series in Gifted Education), (Texas: Prufrock Press, 2006).

Siegle, Ph.D., Del, *The Underachieving Gifted Child: Recognizing, Understanding, and Reversing Underachievement*, (Texas: Prufrock Press, 2012).

Siegle, Del and D. Betsy McCoach, "Making a Difference: Motivating Gifted Students Who Are Not Achieving," *Teaching Exceptional Students*, Sept/Oct 2005.
http://www.gifted.uconn.edu/siegle/publications/TeachingExceptionalMakingADifference.pdf

Gifted Advocates and Consultants

GHF Gifted- & Homeschool-Friendly Professionals
Member-recommended professionals

http://giftedhomeschoolers.org/resources/homeschooling/gifted-homeschool-friendly-professionals/

Melissa Bilash, Advocacy & Consulting for Education
121 North Wayne Ave., Suite 205
Wayne, PA
484-902-4185
http://acfeinc.com

Gail Post, Ph.D., Licensed Psychologist
711 West Ave., Suite 2
Jenkintown, PA
215-884-9260
http://www.gailpost.com

MOOCs: Massive Open Online Classes
MOOCs are free online courses offered to a very large number of people.

Coursera: https://www.coursera.org

edX: https://www.edx.org

Khan Academy: https://www.khanacademy.org

Udacity (Many courses are free, some are for a fee): https://www.udacity.com

Additional Gifted Resources
GHF Favorite Things
   Member-recommended books, resources, and materials
   http://giftedhomeschoolers.org/resources/favorite-things/

Endnotes

Chapter 1

1. Kearney, Kathi, "The highly gifted baby," *Davidson Gifted*, 1993.
http://www.davidsongifted.org/db/Articles_id_10082.aspx

2. Clark, B., *Growing up gifted*, 7th ed. (Upper Saddle River, NJ: Pearson Prentice Hall, 2008), referenced by National Association for Gifted Children, "Traits of Giftedness."
http://www.nagc.org/traits-giftedness

3. Rimm,Ph.D., Sylvia, "So Your Child is Gifted," *Dr. Sylvia Rimm*, 2002.
http://www.sylviarimm.com/article_childgifted.html

4. Silverman, Linda, "What We Have Learned About Gifted Children," *The Gifted Development Center*, 2009.
http://www.gifteddevelopment.com/articles/what-we-have-learned-about-gifted-children

5. Silverman, Linda, "How Parents Can Support Gifted Children," *Gifted Education Digests*, 1992.
http://www.gifted.uconn.edu/siegle/tag/Digests/e515.html

6. "10 Surprising Facts About Albert Einstein," The Huffington Post, October 17, 2013.
http://www.huffingtonpost.com/2013/10/17/abert-einstein-facts_n_3987801.html

7. Gross, Miraca, "Small poppies: Highly gifted children in the early years," *Davidson Gifted*, 1999.
http://www.davidsongifted.org/db/Articles_id_10124.aspx

8. Gross, Miraca, "Small poppies: Highly gifted children in the early years," *Davidson Gifted*, 1999.
http://www.davidsongifted.org/db/Articles_id_10124.aspx

Chapter 3

1. National Association for Gifted Children, "Myths About Gifted Students," *Resources*, accessed January 15, 2015. http://www.nagc.org/resources-publications/resources/myths-about-gifted-students

2. Olszewski-Kubilius, Paula, "Stop Short-Changing Our Most Gifted Students," *The Hill: Congress* Blog, May 3, 2012. http://thehill.com/blogs/congress-blog/education/225289-stop-short-changing-our-most-gifted-children

3. Loveless, Tom, "An Analysis of NAEP Data," Duffett, Ann, and Steve Farkas, "Results from a National Teacher Survey," *High Achieving Students in the Era of NCLB*, (Washington, D.C.: Thomas B. Fordman Insitute, accessed January 2015). http://www.nagc.org/sites/default/files/key%20reports/High_Achieving_Students_in_the_Era_of_NCLB_Fordham.pdf

4. McClarty, Katy, "'They'll be Fine'—Educational Opportunities for Gifted Learners," *Pearson Research and Innovation Network*, March 17, 2014. http://researchnetwork.pearson.com/college-career-success/theyll-fine-educational-opportunities-gifted-learners

5. Zabloski, James, "Gifted Dropouts: A Phenomenological Study," April 20, 2010. http://digitalcommons.liberty.edu/cgi/viewcontent.cgi?article=1356&context=doctoral

6. Streznewski, Marylou Kelly, *Gifted Grown Ups: The Mixed Blessings of Extraordinary Potential*, (New York: John Wiley & Sons, Inc., 1999).

7. Elias, Marilyn, "The School-to-Prison Pipeline: Policies and Practices That Favor Incarceration Over Education Do Us All a Grave Injustice," *Teaching Tolerance*, Spring 2013. http://www.indiana.edu/~pbisin/docs/School_to_Prison.pdf

8. Rodov, Florina and Sabrina Troung, "How some of America's most gifted kids wind up in prison," *Quartz*, December 24, 2014. http://qz.com/317309/how-some-of-americas-most-gifted-kids-wind-up-in-prison/

9. Boodman, Sandra G., "Gifted and Tormented," *The Washington Post*, May 16, 2006. http://www.washingtonpost.com/wp-dyn/content/article/2006/05/15/AR2006051501103.html

10. Lawrence, Julia, "Number of Homeschoolers Growing Nationwide," *Education News*, May 21, 2012.
http://www.educationnews.org/parenting/number-of-homeschoolers-growing-nationwide/

11. Wolfgang, Charlton Hess, "A Phenomenological Investigation Into the Perspectives of Home Schooled Gifted Children and Their Families," May 2013.
https://idea.library.drexel.edu/islandora/object/idea%3A4221/datastream/OBJ/view

12. Ray, Ph. D., Brian D., "Research Facts on Homeschooling," *National Home Education Research Institute*, January 1, 2014.
http://www.nheri.org/research/research-facts-on-homeschooling.html

Chapter 4

1. Post, Ph.D., Gail, "Why some teachers just don't 'get it' about gifted education," *Gifted Challenges*, February 21, 2014.
http://giftedchallenges.blogspot.com/2014/02/why-some-teachers-just-dont-get-it.html

2. "Should child prodigies be allowed to drop out of school?" *USA Today*, May 21, 2013.
http://www.usatoday.com/story/tech/2013/05/21/tech-genius-school/2347289/

Chapter 5

1. Sirkin, Harold, "To Fix U.S. Public Education, Take a Lesson From Countries That Top Student Rankings," *Bloomberg Business Week*, February 4, 2014.
http://www.businessweek.com/articles/2014-02-04/to-fix-u-dot-s-dot-public-education-take-a-lesson-from-countries-that-top-student-rankings

2. Rose, Joel, "How to Break Free of Our 19th-Century Factory-Model Education System," *The Atlantic*, May 9, 2012.
http://www.theatlantic.com/business/archive/2012/05/how-to-break-free-of-our-19th-century-factory-model-education-system/256881/

3. Guisbond, Lisa, "NCLB Crashed and Burned—When Will We Ever Learn?" *Huffington Post Education*, February 5, 2014.
http://www.huffingtonpost.com/lisa-guisbond/nclb-crashed-and-burned-w_b_4731213.html

4. Long, Cindy, "The High-Stakes Testing Culture: How We Got Here, How We Get Out," *NEA Today*, June 17, 2014. http://neatoday.org/2014/06/17/the-high-stakes-testing-culture-how-we-got-here-how-we-get-out/

5. Weller, Chris, "America Hates Its Gifted Kids," *Newsweek*, January 16, 2014. http://www.newsweek.com/america-hates-its-gifted-kids-226327

6. Kantenberger, Dick, "Obama strips all Gifted and Talented and Advanced Placement education funding. What next?" *Examiner*, May 27, 2010. http://www.examiner.com/article/obama-strips-all-gifted-and-talented-and-advanced-placement-education-funding-what-next

7. LoPalo, Tara, "Teaching to the Middle," *Examiner*, January 7, 2011. http://www.examiner.com/article/teaching-to-the-middle

Chapter 6

1. Brasher, Joan, "Are gifted children getting lost in the shuffle?" *Research News @ Vanderbilt*, January 6, 2014. http://news.vanderbilt.edu/2014/01/gifted-children-study/

2. Goodwin, Corin Barsily and Mika Gustavson, *Making the Choice: When Typical School Doesn't Fit Your Atypical Child* (Oregon" GHF Press, 2011), pages 22-24.

3. Price, Pamela, *How to Work and Homeschool: Practical Advice, Tips, and Strategies from Parents* (Oregon: GHF Press, 2013).

4. Davidson, Bob, Jan Davidson and Vanderkam, Laura, *Genius Denied: How to Stop Wasting Our Brightest Young Minds* (New York: Simon & Schuster, 2004).

5. Ray, Brian D., "Research Facts on Homeschooling," *National Home Education Research Institute*, January 1, 2013. http://www.nheri.org/research/research-facts-on-homeschooling.html

Chapter 7

1. Hui, T. Keung, "Home schooling rate accelerates in North Carolina," *News Observer*, August 13, 2014. http://www.newsobserver.com/2014/08/13/4069580_home-schooling-accelerating-in.html?rh=1

2. Delisle Ph.D., James R., *Parenting Gifted Kids* (Texas: Prufrock Press, 2006), page 22.

About the Author

Celi Trépanier was born and raised in south Louisiana. She grew up with a strong Cajun French heritage, eventually married a French-Canadian, and has three wonderful sons. She currently resides in central Iowa with her husband and youngest son.

Celi has a vast and varied background in education. She received her B.S. from Loyola University in New Orleans and her M.Ed. from the University of Louisiana, Lafayette, then taught in Louisiana, Ontario, and Alabama in public schools, private schools, and homeschool co-ops.

Celi became a passionate advocate for gifted children after tiring of her family's painful battles with traditional schools and the misunderstanding and neglect of gifted students. Through adversity came her passion, her strength, and her voice. She advocates for the educational, emotional, and social needs of all gifted children, and her dream is for schools and society to one day understand the truths about giftedness in children. Her writing centers on her advocacy for gifted children and her own journey with her three gifted sons. Her emotional and sometimes pointed posts can be found on her website, Crushing Tall Poppies (crushingtallpoppies.com).